5-28-75

MOEHLER AND BAUR

IN CONTROVERSY, 1832~38:

ROMANTIC-IDEALIST ASSESSMENT

OF THE REFORMATION AND

COUNTER-REFORMATION

AAR STUDIES IN RELIGION
Number Seven

MOEHLER AND BAUR

IN CONTROVERSY, 1832~38:

ROMANTIC-IDEALIST ASSESSMENT

OF THE REFORMATION AND

COUNTER-REFORMATION

by

JOSEPH FITZER

St. John's University, New York City

Tallahassee, Florida
American Academy of Religion
1974

Library of Congress Catalog Card Number: 74-77619

ISBN Number: 0-88420-111-2

Copyright © American Academy of Religion

COMPOSED IN PRESS ROMAN TYPE AT THE CSR EXECUTIVE OFFICE
PRINTED IN THE UNITED STATES OF AMERICA
PRINTING DEPARTMENT, UNIVERSITY OF MONTANA, MISSOULA, MONTANA 59801

CONTENTS

CHAPTER I

Moehler's and Baur's Development Up to 1832

The *Schweizerische Kirchenzeitung* for July 19, 1834, carries the following dispatch:

> Tübingen, July 3, 1834. Möhler's defense of his *Symbolik* against Dr. Baur has just come out, and it is being read with indescribable interest. One would not have believed that in a book primarily polemical in character there could be, along with erudition, such a wealth of practical wisdom. . . . It is clear how fully Möhler is enlivened by the innermost spirit of Christianity: Catholic doctrine shines forth here in such a light as to compel any impartial reader to acknowledge that it is truly divine.[1]

It is good to know that all those people back there in Tübingen were so interested in the pursuit, not only of erudition, but also of practical wisdom. It is good to know, too, that someone back there championed the heavenly origin of Roman Catholic doctrine, or, depending on one's point of view, that someone else had risen up to refute him. For all that, might not the Möhler-Baur controversy better be left to rest quietly in the dust of university libraries? Perhaps— but I think it might actually be useful to step back, take a deep breath, and blow away some dust.

Why? In the first place, though there is certainly no lack of controversial literature between Catholics and Protestants, most of that literature, on closer examination, turns out to be of rather dubious quality. From the breakdown of the Regensburg Colloquy, in 1541, up to the Möhler-Baur controversy, which began in 1832, there is a surprising dearth of really informed and elegant interconfessional discussion. There come to mind the exchanges between Cardinal Bellarmine and the better sort of his Protestant respondents, and between Bossuet and Leibniz, but after noting these one is hard put further to expand the list of serious ecumenical discussions. Similarly, from 1832 up to the present one finds that Catholics and Protestants have been far more concerned with secular culture than with one another. As a result, examination of the Möhler-Baur controversy may well fill a notable gap in the history of ecumenical discussion as well as provide important suggestions for the further conduct of such discussion. For Möhler and Baur *were* informed and elegant. Möhler was the leading light of the *Catholic* Tübingen School, and in his writings he anticipated subse-

---

[1]Quoted in S. Lösch, "J. A. Möhler im Jahre 1834/35," *Tübinger Theologische Quartalschrift,* CVI (1925), 88f. Hereafter this journal will be designated *TQ*. My translation—which will be the case wherever the contrary is not indicated. Note that throughout this study Catholic means Roman Catholic. It should be noted also that this study is a shortened version of my doctoral dissertation, *The Möhler-Baur Controversy, 1832-38,* completed in 1970 at the University of Chicago, under the direction of Prof. B. A. Gerrish. Occasional reference will be made to the longer text, designated *MBC*.

quent Catholic teaching in the areas of development of doctrine, ecclesiology, and, above all, the on-going, organic wholeness of the Catholic liturgy. Baur was the leading light of the *Protestant* Tübingen School, a seminal initiator of the critical study of scripture and church history. Möhler and Baur in controversy offer a paradigm of serious modern ecumenical exchange.

In the second place, and more importantly, perhaps, the late romantics Möhler and Baur introduced a new dimension into the writing of church history. The new dimension consisted in this: both these writers viewed the history and doctrine of the church as unified by a single "all-pervading idea." Möhler and Baur, that is, were concerned not only to contrast Catholic and Protestant views on *particular* points, such as original sin or the authority of the pope, but also to relate the *totality* named "Catholicism" with that named "Protestantism," and furthermore, to demonstrate that, respectively, Catholicism or Protestantism provides the better key for interpreting the wider totality of *all* ecclesiastical history and doctrine. In other words, Möhler and Baur applied to ecclesiastical history a unified restructuring derived from German romantic idealism.[2] To be

---

[2]The best overall survey of the period under consideration is Franz Schnabel's *Deutsche Geschichte im neunzehnten Jahrhundert* (Freiburg im Breisgau, 1929; 4th edition reprinted 1948). The fourth volume of this work is entirely devoted to a study of the religious situation. The best histories of doctrine are, for Catholicism, Karl Werner, *Geschichte der apologetischen und polemischen Literatur* (Schaffhausen, 1861-67; reprinted, Osnabruck, 1966); *idem, Geschichte der katholischen Theologie seit dem Trienter Concil bis zur Gegenwart* (Munich, 1866; reprinted, New York, 1966); and Edgar Hocedez, *Histoire de la théologie au XIX siècle* (Paris, 1947-52); see also L. J. Rogier *et al.*, ed., *Nouvelle histoire de l'église, t, 4, Siècle des lumières, révolutions, restorations* (Paris, 1966), and H. Jedin, ed., *Handbuch der Kirchengeschichte*, Bd. VI/1, *Die Kirche in der Gegenwart: Die Kirche zwischen Revolution und Restauration* (Freiburg/i/B., 1971). An old, but still very useful, survey of German church affairs may be found in G. Goyau, *L'Allemagne religieuse: Le Catholicisme* (Paris, 1905-1909, 4 vols.) and *Le Protestantisme* (Paris, 1906, 1 vol.). For Protestantism, further, one should consult I. A. Dorner, *History of Protestant Theology Particularly in Germany, Viewed According to Its Fundamental Movement and in Connection with the Religious, Moral, and Intellectual Life,* tr. G. Robson and S. Taylor (Edinburgh, 1871); Otto Pfleiderer, *The Development of Theology in Germany since Kant, and Its Progress in Great Britain since 1825,* tr. J. F. Smith (London, 1890); and Emanuel Hirsch, *Geschichte der neuern evangelischen Theologie im Zusammenhang mit den allgemeinen Bewegungen des europaischen Denkens* (Gütersloh, 1949-54). Two valuable short studies are Martin Grabmann: *Die Geschichte der katholischen Theologie seit dem Ausgang der Väterzeit* (Freiburg im Breisgau, 1933; reprinted, Darmstadt, 1960), esp. pp. 192-281; and Martin Kähler, *Geschichte der protestantischen Dogmatik im 19. Jahrhundert,* ed. Ernst Kähler (Munich, 1962).

The attempt to define and meaningfully to use the term *romanticism* is a morass whence the researcher may never return. Perhaps J. L. Talmon, in *Romanticism and Revolt: Europe 1815-1848* (New York, 1967), pp. 135f., has said all that can or need be said: "In Germany, where Romanticism had become a religion, the ecstasies and transports had spent themselves well before 1815, driving not a few of their victims to an early death (Wackenroder, Novalis), to the madhouse (Hölderlin), or to suicide (Kleist). . . . This book has . . . put forward an interpretation of Romanticism as the sum total of the ways in which man's self-awareness was affected by the Revolutionary-Napoleonic disruption, in which he

sure, we are no longer romantic idealists; but Möhler and Baur nonetheless furnish us with highly interesting models for the conscious structuring of church history.

The Möhler-Baur controversy is thus not unworthy of careful reconsideration, for these two thinkers did important, suggestive work in the areas of modern-period ecumenism, church historiography, and historical theology. Documents integral to the controversy are the following:[3]

tried to take his bearings in a world that had lost its 'fixities' and 'definitives'. Man was at once a *révolté* and a creature craving some objective order, a being straining to express and assert itself and a soul yearning for self-surrender." See also Koppel S. Pinson's fine study of nineteenth and twentieth-century Germany, *Modern Germany, Its History and Civilization* (New York, 1966), pp. 1-79. Frederick Copleston, *A History of Philosophy*, VII (New York, 1965), Part 1, 15-49, presents a short summation of the romantic-idealistic mentality: important themes are the sense of the originality of each human person, and of nature as a living organic whole; appreciation of historical continuity and development; and especially the feeling of and longing for the infinite—with the observation that whereas,the romantic pole of the couplet tended to emphasize intuition, the idealistic stressed systematic thought. It is easy to see how, *theologically*, such an outlook would want to repossess the ancient orthodoxies, but yet repossess them after its own fashion. Hence the question arose of how one should appropriate the orthodoxies of the Reformation period, the most recent link with the more remote past. Once appropriated, naturally, the orthodoxies of the Reformation, since they were opposed *then,* led to a re-enactment of the opposition—a salient instance of which re-enactment is the object of the present study. For all that, acquaintance with the theological literature of 1815-48 leaves one with the feeling that this literature actively resists *Wissenschaft*; really to understand, the *accurate* researcher does better to observe Turner and hear Chopin, . . . and buries such a conviction in a footnote!

[3]Möhler's *Symbolik* has appeared in a modern critical edition, ed. Josef Rupert Geiselmann (2 vols.; Cologne and Olten: Jakob Hegner, 1958-60). Vol. I contains Bks. I-II of Möhler's text as it appeared in the fifth (1838) and following editions, together with an introduction by Geiselmann; Vol. I will hereafter be designated *S.* Vol. II contains Geiselmann's critical apparatus, consisting of extensive additional footnotes, a detailed history of the text through its first five editions, and a lengthy doctrinal commentary on the text; Vol. II will hereafter be designated *S-II.* The English translation of the 5th German edition used in the present study is that of James Burton Robertson, *Symbolism: or, Exposition of the Doctrinal Differences between Catholics and Protestants, as Evidenced by Their Symbolical Writings* (3rd ed.; New York: The Catholic Publication House, n.d.). The first edition of Robertson's translation was published in London in 1843. Robertson's text has occasionally been altered to conform to modern standard usage. In particular, Robertson's "symbolism" has been changed to its modern equivalent, "symbolics," or "symbolical theology." In Chap. II of the present study the discussion is based on Geiselmann's modern edition of the *Symbolik,* which, as mentioned above, corresponds to the last (1838) edition prepared by Möhler himself. When there are noteworthy divergences between the 1838 and earlier editions of the *Symbolik* these will be mentioned in the notes. Baur's *Gegensatz* (1st ed.; Tübingen: Ludwig Friedrich Fues, 1834) was brought out by the same publisher, in 1836, in a second edition, "verbesserte, mit einer Uebersicht über die neuesten, auf die Symbolik sich beziehenden, Controversen vermehrte." In general it may be said that the two editions are substantially the same, the second differing from the first in

Möhler, *Symbolik, oder Darstellung der dogmatischen Gegensätze der Katholiken und Protestanten nach ihrer öffentlichen Bekenntnisschriften,* five editions, Mainz, 1832, 1833, 1834, 1835, and 1838;

Baur, *Der Gegensatz des Katholicismus und Protestantismus nach den Principien und Hauptdogmen der beiden Lehrbegriffe, mit besonderer Rücksicht auf Herrn Dr. Möhler's Symbolik,* two editions, Tübingen, 1833-34 and 1836;

Möhler, *Neue Untersuchungen der Lehrgegensätze zwischen den Katholiken und Protestanten: eine Vertheidigung meiner Symbolik gegen die Kritik des Herrn Professors Dr. Baur in Tübingen,* two editions, Mainz, 1834 and 1835;

Baur, "Erwiederung auf Herrn Dr. Möhler's neueste Polemik gegen die protestantische Lehre und Kirche in der Schrift: *Neue Untersuchungen, . . ."* *Tübinger Zeitschrift für Theologie,* VIII (1834:3), pp. 127-248.

some textual emendations (chiefly in pp. 146-73); in the addition of appendices to each of the chapters, which deal with various criticisms of the first edition; in the addition of seven brief appendices at the end of the work, which deal with certain questions of detail; and in the considerable expansion of the introduction (from 15 to 59 pp.).

The present study will make reference principally to the second edition of 1836, in order to present Baur's work in its final form; noteworthy divergences between the editions will be indicated in the notes. Hereafter the first edition will be designated G^1, the second G^2. All translations from G^{1-2} are by the present writer.

Möhler's *Neue Untersuchungen* (Mainz: Florian Kupferberg, and Vienna: Karl Gerold, 1834) was brought out in a second "vermehrte und verbesserte" edition, by the same publishers in 1835. Unfortunately there has not been a modern, critical edition: the Minerva Verlag, Frankfurt a/M., has issued a photocopy (1969) of the 1834 edition. The first and second editions are only slightly different; there are some emendations of the text but no notable additions to it except for Section 26, pp. 127-35, on the Old Testament conception of the origin of evil and sin. Sections 26ff. in the 1834 edition thus correspond to Section 27ff. in the 1835 and subsequent editions. In the present study quotations will be taken from the 1835 edition (designated *NU*).

Baur's "Erwiederung" (*sic*—designated *E*) was also issued separately by Fues (Tübingen, 1834). Because each critic had *his own* axe to grind, a discussion of *contemporary* accounts of the Möhler-Baur controversy would tend to make this study gallop off in all directions. Mention should be made, nonetheless, of the most important of them: P. K. Marheineke, *Über Dr. Johann Adam Möhlers Symbolik oder Darstellung der dogmatischen Gegensätze* (Berlin, 1833); A. Günther, *Der letzte Symboliker* (Vienna, 1834; reprinted, Frankfurt a/M., 1968); anon., *Möhler's Symbolik und ihre protestantisch-symbolischen Gegner* (Mainz, 1835); C. J. Nitsch, *Eine protestantische Beantwortung der Symbolik Möhler's* (Hamburg, 1835); and J. F. E. Tafel, *Vergleichende Darstellung und Beurtheilung der Lehrgegensätze der Katholiken und Protestanten, mit besonderer Rücksicht auf Möhler und seine protestantischen Gegner* (Tübingen, 1835). Marheineke's recension appeared originally in the *Jahrbücher für wissenschaftliche Kritik,* 1833:2; that of Nitsch in *Theologische Studien und Kritiken,* VII (1834) and VIII (1835); and that of the anonymous Catholic in *Der Katholik,* in 1834 (LIV, 245ff.) and 1835 (LV, 39ff.; LVI, 12ff.; LVII, 23ff.).

The present study will therefore take this form: (i) a description of Baur's and Möhler's intellectual development up to 1832; (ii) an examination of the most important sections of Möhler's *Symbolik*; (iii) an examination of the most important sections of Baur's *Gegensatz*; (iv) an examination of the remaining relevant documents; and (v) a brief epilogue.

Baur's Development up to 1832

Ferdinand Christian Baur was born on June 21, 1792, in the village of Schmiden, not far from Stuttgart, the capital of the then Duchy of Württemberg. In 1809, having determined to become, like his father, an evangelical pastor, he enrolled at the seminary attached to the University of Tübingen, the celebrated *Tübinger Stift* that numbered Schelling, Hegel and Hölderlin among its graduates. After a brief period of pastoral work and several lower academic appointments Baur returned to the University in 1826, as *ordentlich* professor of church history, history of dogma, and New Testament studies—a post which he retained till his death in 1860. Since Peter C. Hodgson's recent and readily available study of Baur contains an extended account of his development, it will be necessary here only to touch upon a few points.[4]

The theological instruction to which Baur was exposed from 1809 to 1814 seems to have been an odd, incoherent mixture of traditional supernaturalism with bits of Kantian criticism. It was thus with relief, and even joy, that Baur immersed himself in Schleiermacher's *Die christliche Glaube,* first published in 1821-22. In a long letter to his brother Friedrich August, dated July 26, 1823, Baur describes the impression Schleiermacher's work has made upon him:

> No theological work has as yet appealed to me in so many ways as this one, and, overlooking certain idiosyncrasies of outlook, it contains in every single chapter such a wealth of ideas, and so much by way of improvement of the usual dogmatic views, that it really ought to be given more attention than up to now appears to have been the case. . . . Especially remarkable is the so completely organic plan and development of the system; and then, next to this dialectical skill, how wonderful it is to find the whole penetrated and animated by a genuine religious spirit, something so foreign to the usual dogmatics.[5]

[4]Peter C. Hodgson, *The Formation of Historical Theology: A Study of Ferdinand Christian Baur* (New York, 1966). See also Prof. Hodgson's extended introduction to the volume he has edited and translated for *A Library of Protestant Thought, Ferdinand Christian Baur on the Writing of Church History* (New York, 1968), where he somewhat modifies his earlier assessment of Baur. It should be noted that the present study deals with Baur only up to the end of his involvement with Möhler; Baur's work from 1838 to 1860 is another whole area of inquiry, too broad for inclusion here and too nuanced to be summed up in a simple formula.

[5]There are three extended studies dealing with Baur's life and work: G. Frädrich, *Ferdinand Christian Baur: der Begründer der Tübinger Schule als Theologe, Schriftsteller,*

Organic system and religious spirit together: as a young scholar Baur had apparently been torn between the claims of traditional, if supernaturalist, religiosity and critical, systematic idealism, but now he has found what he was looking for all along. Still, his enthusiasm for Schleiermacher is measured, by no means uncritical.

The *Christliche Glaube*, Baur continues, can be viewed from either a philosophical or a theological point of view. Philosophically, the work seems to be classifiable as idealistic and pantheistic—something like the thought of Spinoza, at least as regards its pantheism. Everything is developed from an analysis of self-consciousness—here is the idealistic side of the system—but still the personality of God and man's freedom of choice seem to be denied. Yet it is difficult to be sure, for

> throughout the work it is Schleiermacher's practice to allow his resolution of
> certain central philosophical questions—upon which his whole system hinges—
> to be guessed at, rather than intentionally to come to terms with them, since
> he means always to remain within the boundaries of theology.[6]

und Charakter (Gotha, 1909)—perhaps the best single work on Baur; Wolfgang Geiger, *Spekulation und Kritik: Die Geschichtstheologie Ferdinand Christian Baurs* (Munich, 1964); and Hodgson, *Formation*. A fourth book on Baur, Ernst Schneider, *Ferdinand Christian Baur in seiner Bedeutung für die Theologie* (Munich, 1909), is no doubt a passable example of what it was meant to be—the winner of a contest for Baur studies—but it is largely derived from other sources and lacking in documentary referencing. Information on the early life and training of Baur is scanty: in addition to the first three of the works just mentioned one should consult Karl Bauer, "Ferdinand Christian Baur als Kirchenhistoriker," *Blätter für Württembergische Kirchengeschichte,* new series XXV (1921), 1-70, XXVI (1922), 1-60; *idem,* "Die geistige Heimat Ferdinand Christian Baur's," *Zeitschrift für Theologie und Kirche,* new series IV (1923), 63-73; *idem,* "Zur Jugendgeschichte von Ferdinand Christian Baur (1805-1807)," *Theologische Studien und Kritiken,* new series XCV (1923-24), 303-13; and, above all, the principal biographical sources, Eduard Zeller, "Ferdinand Christian Baur," *Allgemeine deutsche Biographie* (Leipzig, 1875), II, 172-79, and *idem,* "Ferdinand Christian Baur," *Vortage und Abhandlungen geschichtlichen Inhalts* (Leipzig, 1875), I, 390-479. Zeller was Baur's son-in-law. See also Schnabel, *op. cit.,* IV, 519-23; and K. Klüpfel, ed., *Geschichte und Beschreibung der Universität Tübingen* (Tübingen, 1849). The latter work contains two chapters by Baur, "Die evangelisch-theologische Fakultät vom Jahr 1777 bis 1812," pp. 216-47, and "Die evangelisch-theologische Fakultät vom Jahr 1812 bis 1848," pp. 389-426. It is to be noted that the literature on Baur does not contain any detailed discussion of Baur's controversy with Möhler; ordinarily writers on Baur confine themselves to mentioning that such a controversy did in fact take place.

The letter is reprinted in Heinz Liebing, "Ferdinand Christian Baurs Kritik an Schleiermachers *Glaubenslehre*," *Zeitschrift für Theologie und Kirche,* LIV (1957), 238-43. Quoted, p. 238.

[6]*Ibid.,* p. 238. It is difficult to determine when and to what extent Baur became familiar with Schleiermacher's philosophical doctrines and publications.

Assuming the *Christliche Glaube* to be both idealistic—in the sense of stressing the primacy of self-consciousness—and pantheistic, is it thereby simply self-contradictory? After all, "pantheism cancels out personal freedom and individuality, and idealism posits an absolute freedom." Be that as it may, Baur notes, "the one just as the other system is one-sided and unsatisfying if it be worked out in strict form and continuity." And yet he wavers: "Nonetheless, each has its necessary truth."[7] Baur's answer seems to be, in sum, that the *Christliche Glaube* merely exemplifies the fate of philosophy generally, the affliction of never being able to synthesize apparently conflicting necessary truths. Digressing from Schleiermacher for a moment, Baur sketches his own view of philosophy:

> My view, here, is that, in general, it belongs to the nature of human knowledge to be suspended, undecided, over two thus opposed systems, without being able to attain its completion and true reality in one of them. Hence one must not look upon any system as a static form, but view it rather as an ideal type, with respect to which knowledge is to be conceived only as an approach. Single problems can be resolved only with respect to a determinate option, that is, relatively—not absolutely. Anyway, who would condemn a certain presentation to death for inclining to one system more than another?[8]

Returning to the *Christliche Glaube* Baur observes that

> Schleiermacher, if he seems pantheistically to take away freedom, nonetheless allows the idealistic retort according to which what appears to be pure dependence can be understood as pure action and freedom—although up to now I am not in a position to form for myself a definite idea of how to reconcile the two points of view.[9]

If, however, Schleiermacher's philosophical reticence leaves one as perplexed as before, his emphasis on self-consciousness is, in theology, a great blessing, a great improvement over the sort of theology that Baur was taught at Tübingen. "I know no presentation of Christianity," he says, "in which its essence is so acutely perceived and so thoroughly made the center of the whole system, none that could be held to be more Christian or orthodox."[10] Schleiermacher's superiority lies, of course, in his awareness that the Christian consciousness, instead of being formed according to the gospels (and, by extension, dogmatic commentary upon them), rather recognizes itself in them—and thereby authenticates *them* as Christian. The opposite of Schleiermacher's position can only be "the thoroughly confusing view that religion is the daughter of theology."[11]

[7]*Ibid.*, pp. 239f.

[8]*Ibid.*, p. 240.

[9]*Ibid.*

[10]*Ibid.*

[11]*Ibid.*, pp. 241f.

Yet, once again, Baur's obvious enthusiasm is not without measure. What happens when the theology of self-consciousness attempts to come to terms with the person of Christ? Schleiermacher states that no event is exclusively either natural or supernatural. Christ is God only insofar as in him there existed a perfect God-consciousness, but at the same time he is, as such, the completion of creation. And this *one* Christ may be viewed as both historical and ideal. What happens, Baur notes, is that

> precisely this part of the system appears to me to be the most difficult to understand, the hardest to grasp in the whole of its profound inter-connectedness. If even the most important truths about the person of the redeemer are educed from the religious self-consciousness, if, thus, the exter-nal history of Jesus is taken as a history of the inner development of the religious self-consciousness, I can think of the person of the redeemer only as a certain form of potency of self-consciousness, which form and potency appears in terms of an external history because the natural development of the self-consciousness toward its highest fulfillment at one point had necessarily to take this course. Christ is therefore in each man, and the external appearance of Jesus is not what is fundamental here; rather, in the historical the proto-typical or ideal is supposed to be displayed and the inner consciousness there-by brought to clarity. It is self-evident how exactly this coheres with the pantheistic-idealistic basis of the whole system.[12]

In short, even if Schleiermacher's philosophical theology is *better* than any theology Baur has yet encountered, it *still* fails to resolve serious dialectical tensions. Even though Baur readily admits that theological reflection can only begin with the self-consciousness of the religious believer, he is yet disturbed by the fact that, in Schleiermacher, there is no structure of mediation, philosophi-cally, between self-consciousness and a pantheistically determinate world-order, and, theologically, between self-consciousness and the historical Jesus.

The fact is, Baur's maturation as a religious thinker was achieved in and through dialogue with Schleiermacher.[13] One is thus not surprised to find that Schleiermacher receives considerable attention in his inaugural dissertation at the University of Tübingen, *Primae rationalismi et supernaturalismi historiae capita potiora,* which was delivered in three parts in the course of 1827-28. At the request of the *Tübinger Zeitschrift für Theologie* Baur provided for its readers a German digest of the first two parts of the dissertation; it is this latter text that will now briefly be considered.[14]

---

[12]*Ibid.,* pp. 242f.

[13]Certain items from Baur's early years will not be discussed here because their subject-matter is only incidentally related to inter-confessional controversy. Interesting, however, as illustrating his attitude toward Schleiermacher is Baur's first major work, *Symbol und Mythologie, oder die Naturreligion des Alterthums* (Stuttgart, 1824-25, 3 vols.); see, e.g., I, 104, 157, and II, 363. On the other hand, as Frädrich points out (*op. cit.,* p. 18), this work is not without traces of Schelling's influence.
Schelling's influence.

Baur begins by distinguishing supernaturalism and rationalism. The former, "no matter how much room it allows reason, nonetheless derives everything that necessarily pertains to the religious knowledge and happiness of man from a particular, spontaneous and free divine causality that was operative at a definite time." The latter can be subdivided into the common rationalism of the Enlightenment, "which holds to be the true content of Christianity only that which either was or could have been, through the correct use of reason, the spiritual possession of any period," and what Baur calls "ideal rationalism." This ideal rationalism "recognizes in Christianity something entirely unique and essentially distinct from everything pre-Christian; still, it holds . . . that there cannot be anything purely super-rational or supernatural. Anything with that appearance must be able to be understood in terms of the inner nature of the human spirit."[15] Now, says Baur, as opposed to both the supernaturalism of orthodox Christianity as well as the rationalism of the Enlightenment, the ancient Sabellians along with Schleiermacher (and to some extent Schelling) have professed this ideal, developmental rationalism. Such is the argument of the first two sections of Baur's inaugural dissertation. The dissertation is an interesting document, for it sums up Baur's interests and development up to 1828 just as surely as it foreshadows all his future work. The two foci of his work are the points of comparison in these lectures; the presence of Christian truth in pre-Christian and early Christian religion, and the quest for the modern reappropriation of that truth, as carried out in terms of that acknowledged presence.

As regards Schleiermacher, one finds that the evaluation made of him in the letter of 1823 is not substantially altered but only made more precise. The problem with Schleiermacher's form of ideal rationalism is to be located precisely in Schleiermacher's distinction between dogmatic propositions that refer to (1) the inner states of man, (2) the external world, and (3) the divine attributes. With respect to the first two classes distinguished here, Baur argues,

> Even if, to be sure, the second form ought not be separated from the first, but is rather already radically contained in it, this is still an unsatisfactory definition of the basic principle of Christian dogmatics. Ultimately, in fact, everything depends on whether the second form is in itself independent and self-sufficient and has a necessarily determining influence on the first. According to the place and significance that Schleiermacher gives to the first, however, it is clearly impossible to assume that such is the case. If, moreover, one can name all that forms the opposite of the historical the philosophical (without prejudice to Schleiermacher's entirely correct distinguishing of the philosophical and the religious), it must be said that the historical side of his *Glaubenslehre*

---

[14] *Primae rationalismi et supernaturalismi historiae capita potiora. Pars. I. De gnosticorum christianismo ideali. Pars. II. Comparatur gnosticismus cum Schleiermacherianae theologiae indole. Pars. III. Exponitur praesertim arianismi indoles rationalis.* (Tübingen: Hopfer de l'Orme, 1827-28). In German, "Anzeige der beiden academischen Schriften von Dr. F. C. Baur," *Tübinger Zeitschrift für Theologie,* I (1828), 220-64.

[15] *Ibid.,* pp. 224f.

is wholly subordinated to the philosophical side.[16]

In other words, assuming that historical research can establish some kind of historical Christ, this man can only be he in whom the religious possibilities of mankind are most highly developed, and by whom a society for the sharing of such development has been founded. But "the divine in him can only be the God-consciousness as, in the idea of redemption, attaining to its most perfect self-expression."[17] Man's God-consciousness—Christ's or anyone else's—is a purely inner event. To transfer predicates from what one is inwardly conscious of to what comes to one from the outside—for example, a redeemer and his church—is plainly illogical. Hence the Christ and church of Schleiermacher tend to be devoured by Schleiermacher's fundamental idealism. It is true, of course, that by emphasizing that religion is—if not wholly, nonetheless very importantly—inwardness, Schleiermacher has done a great service for theology. Baur asks only that he would complete what he has begun, by clearly stating the philosophical principles underlying his theology, and then, if he still can, by showing how predicates are to be transferred from states of consciousness to objective, extra-mental realities.[18] Were this to be done no end of problems would be cleared up, above all, that of relating the Christian consciousness to historical redeemer and historical church, and also that of relating that upon which man is absolutely dependent to man's indubitable experience of freedom of choice.[19]

In 1828, then, Baur the religious man and philosopher of religion is convinced of the validity of Schleiermacher's basing religion on the feeling of absolute dependence. On the other hand, Baur the Christian and historian of religion feels uneasy about reducing the historical facticity of Christ and his church to a kind of accident of an exclusively subjective substance of Christianity. It would appear that Baur's uneasiness with Schleiermacher led him, sometime between 1828 and 1833, to make a careful study of Hegel.

Just when Baur began to study Hegel cannot accurately be established, though there is no evidence in those of Baur's works published before 1833 that he had any notable knowledge of or enthusiasm for Hegel's thought.[20] A possi-

---

[16]*Ibid.*, pp. 246f. The reference is to *Die christliche Glaube*, 2nd ed., Sec. 30.

[17]*Ibid.*, p. 251.

[18]*Ibid.*, pp. 240, 247, 251.

[19]*Ibid.*, pp. 258f. Schleiermacher replied to this critique in his *Sendschreiben über seine Glaubenslehre an Lücke*, ed. Hermann Mulert (Giessen, 1908), of which see esp. pp. 54-56, 64-65.

[20]Regarding the point at which Baur became a Hegelian, see Wilhelm Lang, "Ferdinand Baur und David Friedrich Strauss," *Preussische Jahrbücher*, CLX (1915), 476ff. For reasons stated later, p. 97, I cannot agree with Lang that Baur first studied Hegel in the winter of 1834-35. I should add that throughout this study I mean the terms *Hegelian* and *Hegelianism* to refer only to the work of Hegel himself, to what, tongue-in-cheek, one might call "middle Hegelianism," as opposed to "right-wing" or "left-wing" *modifications* of Hegel's views.

ble stimulus to studying Hegel may have been provided by Baur's sometime pupil D. F. Strauss. In the spring of 1832 the young Strauss returned to Tübingen from a sojourn in Berlin, and in that summer he began to lecture on logic and metaphysics in a manner reflecting Hegel's influence upon him. It has been suggested that Baur may have felt it beneath his dignity to come out simply as yet another *Hegelianer*.[21] Be that as it may, the dignity of historical theology as a personal and an academic pursuit called for a solution to the problems raised by the incompleteness of Schleiermacher's work, whereas Hegel's work seemed to merit further examination. It is a safe guess that during his leisure hours in 1832 Baur was making just such an examination.

Möhler's Development up to 1832

Johann Adam Möhler was born on May 6, 1796, in the village of Igersheim, near Mergetheim—roughly fifty miles northeast of Stuttgart.[22] He was the son of a prosperous innkeeper and *Geheimrat*. Having decided, somewhat against his father's wishes, to become a priest, he enrolled, in 1813, in the Catholic seminary of Ellwangen.

[21] See Frädrich, *op. cit.*, pp. xvf., 83, 96; Bauer, "Kirchenhistoriker," p. 19.

[22] As compared to the student of Baur, the student of Möhler is better off in every respect. In the first place, Möhler's own works are for the most part available in excellent modern editions. Secondly, *biographical material* is abundantly available. To begin with, there is the basic source, Stefan Lösch, ed., *Johann Adam Möhler*, Bd. I; *Gesammelte Aktenstücke und Briefe* (Munich, 1928); Bd. II was to be a biography based on Bd. I, but it never appeared. One should also examine Balthasar Wörner, *J. A. Möhler: ein Lebensbild*, ed. P. B. Gams (Regensburg, 1866); F. X. Reithmayr, "Lebensskizze Möhlers," contained in the critical edition of Möhler's *Symbolik*, II, 122-42; *idem.*, "Möhler," in *Wetzer und Weltes Kirchenlexikon* (Freiburg, 1893, 2nd edition), VII, 1677-89; Heinrich Kihn, *Ergänzungen zu Möhler's Symbolik . . . nebst dem Lebensbilde Möhler's*, ed. J. M. Raich (Mainz, 1902); and James Burton Robertson, "Memoir of Dr. Möhler," prefaced to Robertson's translation, *Symbolism . . .* (London, 1843), pp. xxx-ciii. Inaccuracies in the Wörner-Gams biography are corrected in Sebastian Merkle, "Möhler," *Historisches Jahrbuch dder Görresgesellschaft*, LVIII (1938), 249-67. Thirdly, Möhler and the Catholic Tübingen School generally have been the object of excellent *studies*. The most important are Edmond Vermeil, *Jean-Adam Möhler et l'école catholique de Tubingue* (Paris, 1913); Josef Rupert Geiselmann, *Die katholische Tübinger Schule* (Freiburg, 1964); and *idem*, a block of material on Möhler which has been reworked, or merely republished, on several occasions and under several different titles, its most convenient location being "Zur Einfuhrung" and "Sachlicher Kommentar," pp. [13-91] and 585-628 respectively, of Johann Adam Möhler, *Die Einheit in der Kirche, oder das Prinzip des Katholizismus*, ed. J. R. Geiselmann (Cologne: Hegner, 1956), and "Zur Einfuhrung" and "Sachkommentar," I, [15-148]; II, 359-752, of Johann Adam Möhler, *Symbolik, oder Darstellung der dogmatischen Gegensätze der Katholiken und Protestanten*, ed. J. R. Geiselmann (Cologne: Hegner, 1958-60). The first volume of the critical edition of the *Symbolik* contains an introduction by Geiselmann and Möhler's text; the second volume contains, besides Geiselmann's long commentary (largely the same as his book *Die*

To leave Möhler for a moment, it must be kept in mind that in 1803 the territories of the Catholic prince-bishops had been divided up among the adjoining secular states, and thus the rulers of Württemberg had acquired not only the title of king but also a large number of new Catholic subjects, in fact, roughly a third of the population of the new kingdom. To provide for the education of a clergy to serve them—since the institutional basis of German Catholicism had largely been ruined—a seminary had been founded at Ellwangen in 1812; but when, by reason of its isolation, this educational venture proved unsatisfactory, the seminary was incorporated into the University of Tübingen in 1817.[23] The University thus came to have two theological faculties, one Evangelical and one Catholic—an arrangement of considerable import for the subsequent ecclesiastical life and thought not only of Württemberg but of all Germany. From the very start, it may be noted, the new Catholic faculty both could and did take its role very seriously. Unlike the Protestant faculty, whose wavering between supernaturalism and rationalism was to afflict Baur for the first fifteen years of his academic life, the Catholics, particularly Johann Sebastian Drey[24] and Johann Baptist Hirscher, possessed a fairly clear idea of what they wanted and how to achieve it. The ruin of pre-Napoleonic institutional Catholicism had left them free to construct a new, truly German Catholicism, drawing equally on the

theologische Anthropologie Johann Adam Möhlers [Freiburg, 1955]), F. X. Reithmayr's "Lebensskizze" (see above, this note), and a very carefully worked out comparison of the five editions of the Symbolik that Möhler saw through the press. In addition to the works of Vermeil and Geiselmann the following articles should especially be consulted: K. Bihlmeyer, "J. A. Möhler als Kirchenhistoriker, seine Leistungen und seine Methode," TQ, C (1919), 134-98; S. Losch, "J. A. Möhler und die Lehre von der Entwicklung des Dogmas," TQ, IXC (1917-18), 25-59, 129-52; and A. Schmid, "Die Geistige Entwicklungsgang J. A. Möhlers," Historisches Jahrbuch des Görresgesellschaft, XVIII (1897), 322-56, 572-99. A complete bibliography of primary and secondary Möhler sources is to be found in Paul-Werner Scheele, Einheit und Glaube: J. A. Möhlers Lehre von der Kirche und ihre Bedeutung für die Glaubensbegründung (Munich, 1964)—to which, however, must be added S. Losch, Prof. Dr. Adam Gengler:... Ein Lebensbild mit Beigabe von 80 bisher unbekannten Briefen, darunter 47 neuen Möhler-Briefen (Würzburg, 1963). Finally, it must be noted that the Möhler-Baur controversy has been discussed at some length by two writers on Möhler: Vermeil, op. cit., pp. 211-97; and F. Vigener, Drei Gestalten aus dem modernen Katholizismus (Munich, 1926), pp. 37-75—concerning which two discussions see p. 73.

[23]TQ, CVIII (1927) contains two articles on the Catholics at Tübingen: J. Zeller, "Die Errichtung der katholisch-theologischen Fakultät in Tübingen im Jahre 1817," pp. 77-158; and S. Lösch, "Die katholisch-theologischen Fakultäten zu Tübingen und Giessen (1830-50)," pp. 159-208. See also P. Schanz, "Die katholische Tübinger Schule," TQ, LXXX (1898), 1-49, and, in addition, the above-mentioned work of Vermeil.

[24]Regarding Drey's theology, see Vermeil, op. cit.; Geiselmann, Die katholische Tübinger Schule; idem, "Die Glaubenswissenschaft der katholischen Tübinger Schule in ihrer Grundlegung durch Johann Sebastian v. Drey," TQ, CXI (1930), 49-117. It should be noted that the Minerva Verlag, Frankfurt a/M., has undertaken the photographic reprinting of a large selection of the works by Möhler, Drey, Hirscher, and various other nineteenth-century German Catholic thinkers. These men, given the consistently high quality of their theological thought and pastoral sensitivity, have been far too much neglected.

contemporary flowering of German intellectual culture and on the folk piety which had lain, untouched, beneath the Enlightenment. In the first issue of the *Theologische Quartalschrift,* which they founded in 1819 (and which has enjoyed a continuous existence ever since), J. S. Drey set down in mature fashion the art of being at once German-romantic-idealistic *and Catholic* :

> Just as the feeling of being and living is itself first and primordial, instead of being generated by the Cartesian *cogito, ergo sum,* and just as this feeling renews itself with the consciousness of substantial identity in every utterance of the power of life, so the self-knowledge, the self-consciousness of primordial Christianity in Catholicism passes through all the centuries on the basis of the unchangeable *substrata* of an unbroken and ever self-identical objective foundation.[25]

Between two extremes, that of philosophical contemplation, which treats the historically positive as allegory and symbol, and that of rationalistic historical criticism, which regards historical data as elements of a succession of quite discrete riddles—two extremes that in the end come to the same thing, pure subjectivity—

> Catholicism holds fast unchangeably to the essence and form of Christianity in a unique image. This image is its very history, a living and unbroken whole that extends through the whole Christian era. . . . On this as a foundation Catholicism not only permits but even holds as necessary . . . both the philosophical construction and the reflective historical criticism of Christianity. Through the former it forms for itself the science of Christianity, which from time immemorial it has possessed in a form indubitably as rigorous as that of Gnosticism and much more rigorous than that of later heresy. Through the latter it fashions for itself a clear image of each single datum or period in the long course of its development. Thus it satisfies reason, which seeks the highest unity of principles, as well as the legitimate demands of understanding, which busies itself with the individual; above all, though, it answers to the need of an objective faith and a profound reverence for divine revelation.[26]

Drey, then, is a thorough-going supernaturalist.[27] An objective divine revelation is the ultimate criterion of religious truth; and this revelation, first externally given and then, by the activity of the Holy Spirit, implanted into the psychic life, not of the individual, but of the Christian community as a whole, is mediated through the ages by a communally shared consciousness. Revelation, however, is given by God with the understanding that man will, by philosophical and historical research, ever more fully draw out the virtualities of the divine

---

[25]J. S. Drey, "Vom Geist und Wesen des Katholizismus," in J. R. Geiselmann, ed., *Geist des Christentums und des Katholizismus: Ausgewählte Schriften katholischer Theologie im Zeitalter des deutschen Idealismus und der Romantik* (Mainz, 1940), p. 198. It would be very helpful if this out-of-print work were to be reissued.

[26]*Ibid.,* p. 203.

[27]See Geiselmann, *Tübinger Schule,* pp. 15-43. But see also Hermann Brösch, *Das Übernaturliche in der katholischen Tübinger Schule* (Essen, 1962).

communication. There is thus no reason why the German Catholic theologian of 1819 should not allow the freest of dialogues between his German culture and his divinely imparted and sustained sense of Catholicism. Drey's published works and private notebooks reveal that he was quite at home in the world of Schelling and Schleiermacher;[28] at no point, however, does he sacrifice traditional Catholic dogma to new systems of thought. For Drey, German idealism never succeeds in being completely systematic—for then it would take the place of his favorite unifying concept, the Kingdom of God; rather it is a kind of neighborhood dispensary of tools for the better understanding of Catholicism. It is interesting to observe how Drey's group noted the same weakness in Schleiermacher's thought as had Baur: the tension between subjectivity on one hand and Christ and his church on the other. In a sense, the essence of the story told here lies in the fact that whereas Baur gave greater emphasis to subjectivity, Drey emphasized the objective church.[29]

It was in this ambience, then, that Möhler pursued his studies, first at Ellwangen and then at Tübingen. In autumn, 1818, Möhler moved to his bishop's house of studies at Rottenburg, and there, on September 18, 1819, he was ordained a priest. After only a year in parish work he was back in Tübingen as a *Repetent*; in his two years in this capacity he devoted himself to the study of classical philology.

Partly from a dearth of qualified applicants and partly from the government's parsimoniousness, one of Hirscher's (who was dean) and Drey's continuing problems was that of obtaining—and keeping—an adequate instructor in church history.[30] Thus, as a measure of last resort, the would-be classicist found himself, rather to his surprise, appointed *Privatdozent* in church history in autumn, 1822. Needless to say, the very reason why Möhler was appointed was the reason why he was unprepared for the task! At any rate, having been given a grant for travel, he spent from autumn, 1822, till spring, 1823, travelling about Germany, visiting such university lecture halls and libraries as looked helpful to him. The high point of his trip was his encounter with Schleiermacher, Marheineke, and especially Neander in Berlin.[31] In the work of Neander Möhler for the first time saw church history carried out with both more or less careful research into primary sources as well as an endeavor to connect isolated facts into a meaningful, organic whole. Regrettably, Möhler would spend only three weeks in Berlin, but now, at least, he had some idea of how church history ought to be done. In summer, 1823, he began to lecture at Tübingen on church history, patristics, and canon law.

[28]See Geiselmann, "Die Glaubenswissenschaft," pp. 54-66.

[29]Vermeil, *op. cit.,* pp. 103-108.

[30]Bihlmeyer, *op. cit.,* pp. 134-41.

[31]For Möhler's letters describing his trip, see Lösch, ed., *Johann Adam Möhler,* pp. 67-96.

In 1825 there appeared Möhler's first major work, the really delightful treatise, *Die Einheit in der Kirche, oder das Prinzip des Katholizismus, dargestellt im Geiste der Kirchenväter der drei ersten Jahrhunderte.*[32] A little cynically, one might suggest that what Möhler did was to discover the theology of Drey in the writings of the fathers. It can hardly be denied, in any case, that the fathers are pressed into service—usually, it must be said, fairly convincingly—as witnesses to the truth of what Möhler learned from Drey. A sampling of the theses that stand at the heads of the chapters will give some idea of the structure and content of the treatise:

> The imparting of the Holy Spirit is the condition of the reception of Christianity in us; he unites all the faithful into a spiritual community, by means of which he imparts himself to those who are not yet among the faithful: inner tradition; Christ is communicated through love, which is generated in us by the reception of the higher spiritual life that holds sway in the Church; only in the community of the faithful do we become conscious of Christ.

> Christian doctrine is the expression of the Christian spirit in terms of concepts.

> Heretics, ecclesiastical egoists, . . . reject and mutilate the holy scriptures and interpret them without the spirit of the Church: the rationalistic principle of interpretation.

> The Church is the external, visible form of a holy, living power, love, which the Holy Spirit imparts; the Church is the body belonging to the spirit of the faithful, a spirit that forms itself from inward out. The hypothesis of an invisible church occurs only in a religion of ideas.

> The diocese: its center is the bishop, the personal representation of the love of the community.[33]

Quite plainly there are many similarities between the ecclesiology outlined here and that of Schleiermacher. Doctrinal statements and ecclesiastical institutions proceed, so to say, *outward* from the Christian consciousness—as opposed to *inward* from "authorities."[34] Still, there are salient differences, the most

[32]See p. 11, n. 22.

[33]Pp. [9f.].

[34]Möhler's discussion of the externals of Catholicism as proceeding outward from the shared consciousness of the community has been a stumbling block for several generations of Catholic scholars. But with what reason? In his preface to the *Einheit* Möhler writes, p. 3: "The treatise . . . begins with the Holy Spirit. Now it may seem odd that I have not begun rather with Christ, the center of our faith. . . . The Father sends the Son, and the Son sends the Spirit: thus did God come to us; we reach God in the reverse manner: the Holy Spirit leads us to the Son, and the Son leads us to the Father. My intention was thus simply to begin with what is temporally first in our becoming Christian." See M. J. Congar, "Sur l'évolution et l'interprétation de la pensée de Möhler," *Revue des sciences philosophiques et théologiques,* XXVII (1939), 205-12.

important of them being that Möhler, far more, it would seem, than
Schleiermacher, stresses the transcendence of the Holy Spirit. There is never a
moment's doubt that for Möhler the Spirit is, even as ground of the Christian
consciousness, wholly transcendent of and distinct from the Christian
community.[35]

The nerve of *Die Einheit in der Kirche* is Möhler's definition of the principle
of this unity: "It consists of life, a life that is immediately and always moved by
the divine Spirit, a life that maintains itself and progresses through the reciprocal
love of the faithful."[36] The individual Christian's test of whether he truly
possesses this divine life is "the identity of the Christian consciousness of the
individual . . . with the consciousness of the whole Church."[37] In view of the
overall problematic of the present study it must now be asked how Möhler, as a
historian, viewed the Christian past. If the ultimate criterion of religious truth is
mediated through a necessarily self-identical conscious life, how is one to do
church history or history of doctrine? To put it another way, if the historian can
know that of which he is the historian only by sharing its life, how will this
circumstance affect his work precisely as history?

Möhler was a prolific writer, and it is impossible to review all the pertinent
documents here.[38] The desired information, however, is easily to be had from
what is undoubtedly the single most pertinent document, the introduction of
Möhler's lectures in church history for the 1826-27 academic year. In his splen-
did anthology of German Catholic writers of the romantic-idealist period, *Geist
des Christentums und des Katholizismus,* J. R. Geiselmann has published these
pages under the title, "Die Idee der Geschichte und Kirchengeschichte."[39]

History, then, is to be defined objectively as "the life of mankind developing and forming itself in time under the guidance of Providence." Subjectively, it
is "the reconstruction of life, an ideal repeating of life in the mind." The two
factors of the product *objective* history are, it can be said, divine and human
freedom, even if "man, as a thoroughly relative being, one burdened with fini-

---

[35]*Die Christliche Glaube,* 2nd ed., Sec. 121.

[36]*Einheit,* Sec. 7, p. 21.

[37]*Ibid.,* Sec. 12, p. 39.

[38]Items relevant to the present discussion in addition to those considered in the text
are: (1) two reviews of books: "G. B. Winer, *Comparative Darstellung des Lehrbegriffs der
verschiedenen christlichen Kirchen-Parteien,* Leipzig, 1824," *TQ* (1826), 111-38, and "A.
Gengler, *Über das Verhaltnis der Theologie zur Philosophie,* Landshut, 1826," *TQ* (1827),
498-522; and (2) Möhler's own large-scale study *Athanasius der Grosse und die Kirche seiner
Zeit* (Mainz, 1827 reprinted, Frankfurt a/M, 1971), esp. pp. 304-25. Möhler here discusses
Schleiermacher's Sabellianism, concluding that Schleiermacher, with his understanding of
religion, is a poor judge of authentic church tradition, cannot really distinguish God and the
world, and must therefore regard the church itself as divine. Möhler's books, it may be added,
had the usual effect: in 1826 he was made *professor extraordinarius*; in 1828 he was made
ordinarius and doctor of theology.

[39]Geiselmann, ed., *Geist,* pp. 391-96; see also Geiselmann's notes, pp. 483-91.

tude, needs to be stimulated and worked on from the outside in order to rise to the level of spontaneity and freedom."[40] Although, therefore, historical understanding (*Verstand*) must examine the individual events of objective history, the real crown of *subjective* historical reason (*Vernunft*) is the relating of historical events first to patterns of free human causality, and, ultimately, to the divine causality that leads man and sustains him. The spiritual nature of man, the complex of the laws of his being, demands this effort at establishing causal relationships; it cannot rest with the so-called "pragmatic" historical style of the Enlightenment. "The laws of reason demand . . . something eternal that will stand over the temporal; they demand that the divine be grasped in the human. This is the religious understanding of history." Simply, then, by reason of its effort to be coherent, subjective history must become religious, must relate events to their divine ground. "According to his spirtual constitution man may be expected to act freely and be the originator of a series of happenings—and what is so for the individual is so for the whole of humanity; but the deity may be expected to bind all things into one whole and lead them harmoniously to one goal."[41] Subjective history, in a word, must recognize the true, even if not immediately evident, structure of its object.

Even if all history is religious, however, one can distinguish between the history of man's specifically religious powers and self-expressions, or church history, and the history of his other accomplishments, or political history. It must be borne in mind, of course, that neither kind of history occurs in isolation from the other. It is in this sense that Christ can be said to be the center of all objective history, and a similar centrality is to be accorded the means of salvation which Christ has instituted. Church history thus becomes the highest type of history. Church history, then, is, "in the objective sense, the Christian life as development, forming itself, or unfolding in time; in the subjective sense, it is the presentation of this development and unfolding." The ultimate reason for the priority given to church history is that, through Christ, "with Christianity a wholly new life came to a large part of humanity."[42]

In order to conduct the study of history "philosophically,"[43] or in accordance with man's reason, a certain procedure must necessarily, preferably intentionally, be followed:

> Anyone who wants to write a real history must proceed from a unity, be it conscious or unconscious, from a basic thought that penetrates the whole, a thought that undergirds everything and permits everything to be understood, a thought to which everything is related and which binds all individuals into a true organism. Indeed, every history is the description of a life, and it is this

---

[40]*Ibid.*, p. 391.

[41]*Geist*, p. 392.

[42]*Ibid.*, p. 393.

[43]The word is Möhler's, *ibid.*

determinate inner power of life, this definite uniqueness, that organically unfolds. For this reason all events in a certain history stand in a dynamic relationship to the unique life-principle.[44]

With respect to church history, then, what precisely is this unity, or better, idea of unity, that one must have in mind?

> It is none other than this: Christ in the Holy Spirit works in the faithful and binds them to unity. The unity of Christian life, therefore, the fact that all the faithful form in Christ a collective life, seems to us to be the unique true idea [of church history]. For the idea must ever seek to strive after the highest, but the goal that the Church is to attain is not attained in any temporal period; if the idea were to enter wholly into time, time itself would be annihilated, the goal of the entire temporal life of the Church being thereby attained.[45]

The idea of church history "must have the character of eternity."[46] In no sense, however, does this bond of unity of objective church history become a subjective *a priori*. The church historian will succeed only if he has *appropriated* this idea subjectively. Primarily, though, the idea is objective. Indeed, the combination of the idea with purely temporal conditions and relationships results in the periodization of church history. Möhler sees four such periods: (1) that of the development of the unity of the Christian life, roughly from the first to the sixth centuries; (2) that of the assimilation of this unity by the barbarian nations, roughly from the sixth to the sixteenth centuries; (3) that of the breaking down of this unity, from the sixteenth century to the present; and (4) that of the return to unity, or the final consummation and its foreshadowings. With respect to the second and third periods Möhler remarks that since the barbarians could become Christian only by the exercise of strong authority, particularly that of the pope, it was natural that there be a reaction, since it is the destiny of Christian man to be free in the church. Carried to excess, though, this desire for Christian freedom became egoistic capriciousness and led to the Reformation. Still, since

> the idea of the Church, the unifying spirit that rules it, demands that we await liberation from this state, that we assume a regeneration to be coming. The third age can hence be considered and treated as a point of transition to a fourth age. . . . Precisely then will freedom and necessity be reconciled.[47]

As a church historian, then, Möhler holds that subjective history, by its very nature, is religious, that is, that it seeks the divine ground of human life. Now

[44]*Ibid.*

[45]*Ibid.*, pp. 393f. See also the Winer review, p. 117.

[46]*Ibid.*, pp. 394-96.

[47]*Ibid.*, p. 396.

the divine ground of man's religious life, and therefore of the entirety of his life, is manifested in Christ: as a result the formality by which church history objectively exists and under which it is subjectively to be viewed is the collective life in Christ of the faithful. Because of the certainty of the divine covenant, moreover, even necessary disruptions of that unity must be seen as purely transitional. Simply to be true to its nature, then, subjective history generally, and *a fortiori* church history, must work in part from supernaturally revealed principles—at least if it is to be *wholly* what it can and should be. And with this conclusion, it may be noted, one can now see the full force of Drey's and Möhler's opting for the church instead of self-consciousness. Even history, normally considered a religiously neutral undertaking, must be, if it is to be the history of what *really* happened, what one might call theological history, or even historical theology.[48] The ultimate resolution of Schleiermacher's dilemma lies in the submission of subjectivity in general, and subjective history in particular, to the ultimate object of historical research.

Partly as a result of what he had seen and heard in his travels, particularly at the Universities of Göttingen and Berlin,[49] and partly no doubt, as a result of the religious situation in Württemberg, Möhler began in the summer semester of 1830 to lecture on an aspect of church history new to German Catholic circles, namely, symbolics, or the comparative study of the Christian *symbola,* or confessions. In 1832 he published a developed version of his lectures under the title *Symbolik, oder Darstellung der dogmatischen Gegensätze der Katholiken und Protestanten.* In his preface to the work Möhler states his reasons for publishing his lectures on symbolics.[50] In the first place—given the revival of confessional Protestantism, a result of the confluence of orthodox-Evangelical, pietist, and governmental interests—it is more than ever necessary that the Catholic clergy and public be accurately informed as to confessional differences between Catholics and Protestants. In the second place, to go to the heart of the

---

[48]J. S. Drey, *Kurze Einleitung in das Studium der Theologie* (Tübingen, 1819; reprinted, Frankfurt a/M., 1966), p. 131n., expressed himself a little more clearly: "It is not the function of the historian as such to serve as a critic . . . of anything new that arises [that is, in the history of religion], but simply to present its causes and effects. If he does the former, he becomes a dogmatician." Möhler is evidently thinking along dogmatic lines in these lectures, where it is his intention to discuss *ultimate* causes and effects.

[49]Noteworthy were G. J. Planck (Göttingen), *Geschichte der Entstehung, der Veränderungen und der Bildung des protestantischen Lehrbegriffs von Anfang der Reformation bis zur Einführung der Concordienformel* (Leipzig, 1781-1800); P. K. Marheineke, *Institutiones symbolicae* (Berlin, 1812); and *idem, Christliche Symbolik, oder historisch-kritische und dogmatische komparative Darstellung des katholischen, reformatorischen und sozinianischen Lehrbegriffs,* 3. Teile, I. Bd., *Das System des Katholizismus* (Heidelberg, 1810). The format of Möhler's *Symbolik* is very similar to that of Marheineke's *Institutiones,* except that Marheineke begins with the doctrine of the church.

[50]*S,* pp. 3-13. See Schnabel, *op. cit.,* pp. 379ff., *passim,* esp. 468-72.

matter, "there can be no solid acquisition, nor confident use of the arguments for any communion, unless they be conceived in relation to the antagonist system."[51] Thus both Catholic and Protestant theologies are, *ipso facto,* "ecumenical." Neither Catholics nor Protestants can understand even *themselves* except in terms of their *Doppelgänger.* The way to an evenual reunion of the churches must therefore begin, paradoxically, with the recollection of sixteenth-century differences. But, by renewing sixteenth-century debate from his nineteenth-century vantage point, Möhler initiated the controversy that is the object of the present study.

---

[51]*S,* p. 4, Eng. tr., p. xx.

CHAPTER II

Moehler's Symbolik

Möhler's *Symbolik* is a large-scale work divided into two books. Book I, after a general introduction to symbolics, compares Catholic, Lutheran, and Reformed teaching in the areas of original justice and original sin; justification, faith and good works; and sacraments, church and eschatology. Book II deals with "the smaller Protestant sects," namely the Radical Reformers, and the Quakers, Pietists, Methodists, Swedenborgians, Socinians and Arminians. The compass of the present study makes an examination of the whole work impossible; but the purpose of this study also makes it unnecessary, for what is chiefly of interest here is Möhler's systematic-deductive approach to historical theology, his effort to see everything in terms of "one all-pervading idea." Baur, moreover, made no attempt to defend the smaller sects, but only the Lutheran and Reformed churches. This chapter will therefore consider what is most basic to Möhler's approach and what chiefly elicited Baur's response, namely, Möhler's views on symbolics generally, on original justice and original sin, and on "Protestantism" as a system of life and thought.

The Nature of Symbolics

The introduction to Book I of the *Symbolik* begins with Möhler's definition of symbolics:

> By symbolics we understand the scientific exposition of the doctrinal differences among the various religious parties opposed to each other in consequence of the ecclesiastical revolution of the sixteenth century, as these doctrinal differences are evidenced by the public confessions or symbolical books of those parties. [1]

By way of explaining this definition Möhler notes, first, that symbolics is fundamentally neither polemical nor apologetic in character. [2] Its function is only to make as clear as possible the doctrinal differences between the various Christian communions. Indirectly, however, symbolics does assume a somewhat controversial appearance, "for the personal conviction of the writer will involuntarily appear and be heard, sometimes in the tone of adhesion and commendation, sometimes in the tone of reproof and contradiction." Still, this introduc-

---

[1] *S*, p. 17 (Eng., p. 1).
[2] *S*, pp. 17f.

tion of a personal element into the discussion in no way runs counter to the nature of symbolics. In this respect symbolics is similar to history, "in which the historian does not conceal his own personal opinion respecting the personages brought forward and the facts recounted."[3] Moreover, as is also the case with history, it can even be said that without this personal element symbolics would be superficial and unscientific:

> A bare narrative of facts, even when accompanied with the most impartial and most solid historical research, will not suffice; nay, the individual proportions of a system of doctrine must be set forth in their mutual concatenation and their organic connexion. Here, it will be necessary to decompose a dogma into the elements out of which it has been formed and to reduce it to the ultimate principles whereby its author had been determined; there, it will be expedient to trace the manifold changes which have occurred in the dogma: but at all times must the parts of the system be viewed in their relation to the whole and be referred to the fundamental and all-pervading idea.[4]

The personal outlook of the historian or symbolist, therefore, is precisely what enables him to unify the bare facts before him into a whole. Any plunge into the depths underlying the factual surface of history is necessarily a personal plunge; only a personal, if unavoidably partial, intuition of "the fundamental and all-pervading idea" can effect the magic transformation of narration into history in the true sense. In a deep and living penetration of the essence of the Christian confessions "the relation of these to the gospel and to Christian reason must necessarily be brought out, and the conformity of the one, and the opposition of the other, to universally acknowledged truths must follow as a matter of course." In other words, the truth will out; and if a certain Christian confession is at variance with the ultimate truth of things, then a properly conducted study of the various confessions will make that deficiency manifest. Of course, when a symbolist thus draws attention to deficiencies he takes on the appearance of a simple controversialist, even if to do so is not his intention. "In this way, indeed," concludes Möhler, "symbolics becomes the most cogent apology, or allusive refutation, without designing to be, in itself, either the one or the other."[5]

The second remark Möhler wishes to make concerning his definition of symbolics bears on the subject matter of this discipline.[6] Symbolics, at least in the context within which Möhler intends to write, is the study of the creedal documents occasioned by the religious upheaval of the sixteenth century. Symbolics is not, therefore, the study either of those doctrinal disputes that took place before the sixteenth century or of the contemporary differences

[3]*Ibid.*

[4]*S*, pp. 17f. (Eng., pp. 1f.).

[5]*S*, p. 18 (Eng., p. 2).

[6]*S*, pp. 18-22.

between western and eastern Christianity. Symbolics deals with the confessions of faith arising out of the Reformation; and within these confessions, moreover, it centers on what Möhler considers to be particularly characteristic of western Christianity, what he terms "the western question." Whereas "the eastern question" is concerned with Christology, the western question "regards exclusively Christian anthropology; for it will be shown that, whatever things may be connected with this, they are all mere necessary deductions from the answer given to the anthropological question mooted by the Reformers."[7] With respect to symbolics as here defined and delimited, therefore, the sought-for "fundamental and all-pervading idea" is clearly going to be a conception of man in relation to Christianity. The Reformation took place because certain western Christians opposed a new understanding of man's condition and prospects to the understanding that had hitherto obtained. More precisely, then, the role of symbolics is to elucidate and to test the varieties of Christian anthropology.

In the third place, Möhler observes, his definition of symbolics emphasizes doctrine, to the relative exclusion of other aspects of ecclesiastical life.[8] It would doubtless be interesting to compare western Christian communions in other ways, for example, with respect to liturgy or even statistics. The fact remains, however, that the principal cause for the division of western Christendom is doctrinal; if it is to fulfill its task, symbolics must attend primarily to the basic options in Christian anthropology and their consequences.

In the fourth place, therefore, Möhler states that the proper sources for symbolics are the various western Christian confessions.[9] Among the relevant confessions are, of course, to be numbered the official documents of the Council of Trent as well as the principal Lutheran and Reformed confessions. In a secondary, derivative sense the writings of the Mennonites, Quakes, Methodists, and Swedenborgians can be counted among the documents relevant to symbolics, because these groups rendered more explicit what was already contained in the Lutheran and Reformed Confessions. Similarly, in the sense that they can be considered a conflicting extreme within Protestantism, the Arminians and Socinians have a claim to be considered. On the other hand nominally Protestant rationalists and Saint-Simonians do not have such a claim, since for them, in a manner not unlike the Muslims, Jesus Christ is simply one among many great teachers of humanity, not a being of unique and transcending import. All of

---

[7]*S*, pp. 18f. (Eng., p. 2).

[8]*S*, p. 22.

[9]*S*, pp. 22-43. The confessional documents to be considered in the *Symbolik* are, from the Roman Church, the canons and decrees of Trent, the *Catechismus Romanus* (with the qualification that it is not strictly a confessional document but only a noteworthy authority), the Tridentine Profession of Faith, and the anti-Jansenist bulls of Innocent X and Clement IX (see *S*, pp. 31-36). From the various Protestant churches Möhler lists a large number of documents (see *S*, pp. 36-43); in fact, however, he relies chiefly on the Lutheran *Book of Concord*.

these smaller or later groups, in any case, will be duly considered in Book II of the *Symbolik*. Book I, as already noted, deals only with the Catholics, the Lutherans, and—to a markedly lesser extent—the Reformed. Now, continues Möhler, there is an extremely important difference between the Catholic confession of Trent and the various Protestant confessions.

To clarify this difference, Möhler asks, to what degree is acquaintance with the writings of individual theologians helpful, and perhaps even *necessary,* if one is to obtain a truly deep and living knowledge of the various public creedal documents? In order to come to such a knowledge of the official teaching of Trent the writings of such individuals as Sarpi and Bellarmine are unquestionably helpful, but, strictly speaking, they are not necessary. They are not strictly necessary because Catholic doctrinal thought, be it public or individual, is essentially a communal undertaking. Since Catholic theologians

> found the dogmas on which they enlarge, which they explain or illustrate, *already pre-existing,* we must in their labours accurately discriminate between their special and peculiar opinions and the common doctrine declared by the Church and received from Christ and the apostles. As these doctrines existed *prior to* those opinions, so they can exist *after* them, and can therefore be scientifically treated *without* them, and quite *independently* of them.[10]

The Catholic theologian is, as such, essentially a commentator upon the already given. Some of his speculation, it is true, may eventually find its way into the *formulation* of official dogma, but in this case it must then be clearly distinguished from other ideas of his that did not furnish the material for solemn papal or conciliar pronouncements; Augustine is a good example of this situation. Catholic dogma is in no sense the creation of one or more individual minds. Rather, even when necessarily expressed in the formulations of certain individuals, it must be understood as the cognitive reflex of the communal life of the Roman Church. The only real basis of Roman Catholic dogma is the religious consciousness of Roman Catholics, in so far as these Catholics are at one with the Word of God proclaimed in their communion. Research into the history of doctrine has only the strictly ancillary function of showing how that consciousness reacted to external stimuli or spontaneously developed according to its own inner law. In Catholicism—and for that matter, only in Catholicism—the communally shared consciousness gives birth to that of the individual:

> This distinction between individual opinion and common doctrine presupposes a very strongly constituted community, based at once on history, on life, on tradition, and is only possible in the Catholic Church. But, as it is possible, so also it is necessary . . . .[11]

In Protestantism it is entirely different. Acquaintance with the writings of

[10]*S,* p. 25 (Eng., p. 7).

[11]*Ibid.*

individuals such as Luther, Zwingli, and Calvin is not merely useful but absolutely necessary for understanding the various confessions. In as much as Möhler's cónception of the relationship between individual and public writings in Protestantism strongly colors his whole exposition of Protestant doctrine, the text of the *Symbolik* will be quoted here at some length. As Möhler sees them then,

> the relation, namely, wherein the Reformers stand to the religious belief of their followers is of a very peculiar nature, and totally different from that of Catholic teachers to Catholic doctrine. Luther, Zwingli, and Calvin are *the creators* of those religious opinions prevalent among their disciples, while no Catholic dogma can be referred to any theologian as its author.[12]

Luther, personally, holds a special place as the very creator of the whole system of religion that is known as "Protestantism":

> As in Luther the circle of doctrines which constitute the peculiar moral life of the Protestant communities was produced with the most independent originality, as all who stand to him in a spiritual relation, like children to their parents, and on that account bear his name, draw from him their moral nurture and live on his fulness, so it is from him we must derive the most vivid, profound, and certain knowledge of his doctrines.[13]

Because, then, of the relationship between Lutheranism in particular—and Protestantism in general—and the personal teaching of Luther, the study of Lutheranism or Protestantism perforce becomes the study of Luther himself:

> The peculiar emotions of his spirit, out of which his system gradually arose, or which accompanied its rise; the higher views, wherein often, though only in passing, he embraced all its details as well as traced the living germ out of which the whole had by degrees grown up; the rational construction of his doctrine by the exhibition of his feelings; all this is of high significancy to one who will obtain a genuine scientific apprehension of Protestantism as a doctrinal system, and who will master its leading, fundamental principle. The Protestant articles of faith are so livingly interwoven with the nature of their original production in the mind of Luther and with the whole succession of views which filled his soul that it is utterly impossible to sever them. The dogma is equally subjective with the causes which co-operated in its production, and has no other stay nor value that what they afford.[14]

Möhler readily concedes that by no means all that is to be found in the writings of the individual reformers eventually made its way into the Protestant confessions. The selectivity of the writers of the confessions, however, was due

[12]*S*, pp. 23f. (Eng., p. 6).
[13]*S*, p. 24 (Eng., p. 6).
[14]*S*, p. 24 (Eng., pp. 6f.).

less to a true scientific concern for purity of doctrine than to the occasional nature of these documents:

> For this religious party was generally satisfied with the results of that process of intellectual generation whereby its doctrines had been produced; and, separating by degrees those results from their living and deepest root, it rendered them thereby for the most part unintelligible to science; as the bulk of mankind are almost always contented with broken, unsubstantial, and airy theories.[15]

It is therefore the task of scientific symbolics, which seeks the fundamental and all-pervading idea of Protestantism, to put Protestantism back together again, to restore to common consciousness the relation between cause and effect, basis and superstructure. And to do this it must go beyond the Protestant confessions; to make these latter comprehensible as a system and in depth "the writings of Luther, and in a relative degree, of the other Reformers, are to be sedulously consulted."[16] For symbolics, then, in addition to the confessions, the writings of the original, individual Protestant theologians are in the most rigorous sense, not adjuncts, but sources.

Thus far, of course, Möhler has concerned himself only with the writings of those individual Protestant theologians who wrote before the confessions were composed. What, on the other hand, is to be said of Protestant theologians who, like Bellarmine among the Catholics, did their theologizing after the confessions? Are they adjuncts or sources? The unfortunate truth is that they are neither; in a word, they cannot be trusted. The problem is not too serious with theologians like Chemnitz and Gerhard, and in fact Möhler will not infrequently refer to their writings. From more recent theologians, however, little can be expected. Protestantism began with individualism; and individualism has so characterized it subsequently that no individual can safely be taken as representative of the community, if, indeed, one can speak of a Protestant community of faith in any more than a purely statistical (or sociological) sense. From the beginning Protestantism is simply "an individuality exalted into a generality"; later generations of Protestants have simply carried on the Reformers' habit of identifying the way they feel about dogmas with the dogmas themselves. In Luther, the first Protestant, remarks Möhler,

> it was the inordinate pretension of an individuality which wished to constitute itself the arbitrary centre round which all should gather—an individuality which exhibited itself as the universal man in whom every one was to be reflected—in short, it was the formal usurpation of the place of Christ, who undoubtedly as individual represents redeemed humanity . . . .[17]

[15]S, p. 25 (Eng., p. 7).

[16]Ibid.

[17]S, pp. 26f. (Eng., p. 8).

Luther's followers did the same as their master: "Every one considered himself . . . the representative of humanity, redeemed from error at least—as a sort of microcosmic Christ."[18] But since each was now his own Christ, there was no longer a common redeemer, no longer a community of faith, and no longer a common dogmatics. Needless to add, the writings of post- confessional Protestant theologians are in no sense sources for symbolics; even their use as adjuncts must be undertaken with extreme caution.

The modern reader may well wonder at this point whether Möhler's original assertion of the scientific impartiality of symbolics is anything but a pious fraud. (As will presently be seen, Baur, too, was rather taken aback with the introduction of the *Symbolik*.) If at the very outset Möhler describes Protestantism as the apotheosis of Luther's ego can he seriously mean to conduct an impartial, scientific comparison of Catholicism and Protestantism? Paradoxically, perhaps, the answer seems to be Yes. In fairness to Möhler one must endeavor to grasp exactly what he is trying to do. The *Symbolik* is not an exercise in the polite ecumenism of the twentieth century.

At no time does Möhler claim to regard the history of Protestantism as anything but the history of an aberration. The kind of open-minded impartiality he calls for is the kind that is no respecter of persons. He will yield to the feelings neither of Protestants, who think Protestantism ought to be treated sympathetically, nor of his fellow Catholics, many of whom still think Protestantism ought to be attacked. Protestantism must speak for itself; and if the speech of its creedal documents is faltering, self-contradictory, and ultimately rooted in the feelings of Luther, well, so much the worse for Protestantism! Möhler readily admits, it will be remembered, that his search for an explication of the idea of Protestantism will accidentally take on an apologetic and polemical tone. But that is the fault of Protestantism, not his fault. Open-minded symbolics is not merely descriptive; it is a search for the ultimate truth and, come what may, an evaluation of contending claims to ultimate truth. With point of view and sources clearly in mind, then, it is time to take a closer look at Protestantism, more precisely, to compare Protestant Christian anthropology with its Catholic counterpart.

Original Justice and the Origin of Evil

The first chapter of Möhler's comparison of Catholic and Protestant Christian anthropology is devoted to the state of man before the fall and to the origin of evil. Möhler is nevertheless well aware that these areas of doctrinal enquiry were not the primary concern of the Reformers; the central issue of the Reformation was justification. He feels called upon to explain why he has chosen to begin his comparison the way he has.

[18]*S*, p. 27 (Eng., p. 8).

Depending on whether one's point of view is Catholic or Protestant, he says, the entire history of either a single man or all mankind will look different.[19] If human life, both in the individual and in the race, is an organic unity, it follows that absolutely no moment in human life can be seen independently of one's confessional perspective, least of all Adam's first moments in the Garden of Eden. Because of the unity of what is there to be seen, to see any given moment of human life from a certain point of view is implicitly, at least, to see every moment of human life from that point of view.

On the other hand, it was by no means evident at the beginning of the Reformation that the Reformers' doctrine of justification was in fact the basis of a new understanding of the totality of human life. No revolution, civil or ecclesiastical, is brought about in terms of a completely developed system of thought. What happens, rather, is that the fundamental principles of a revolution are first lived; only later do they become fully conscious. Thus the Reformers did not immediately perceive that their doctrine about how fallen man achieves union with Christ would have important consequences in other areas of doctrine. Only after a certain amount of time and experience did the Reformers' central doctrine of justification expand both backward and forward, so to speak, including thereby the beginnings of the human race as well as its life after death.

Like human life itself, the doctrinal system of Catholicism is an organic whole, so that an attack at one point is necessarily an attack on the whole system. The fact that the Reformers began by questioning the Catholic doctrine of justification is much less important than the fact that the inner logic of their perspective forced them to attack the entire system of Catholic life and thought. What time and experience brought them was the consciousness that one complete system can be opposed only by another complete system. Even if the doctrine of justification was and remains the central area of opposition between Catholics and Protestants, Möhler concludes, the systematic inclusiveness of that opposition makes it possible to begin the comparison of the two religious systems at another, more logical point. Möhler chooses the doctrine of the original state of man, or original justice, because, he says, the simplest form of exposition is to follow step by step the progress of human history.

The moment of original justice, the first step in human history, is hidden from the inspection of man's reason. Only divine revelation can teach man both what he once was and now truly is. Revelation does this through the doctrine of the restoration of man to his original righteousness, which restoration is brought about through Jesus Christ. From what man is, through Jesus Christ, to become, he can learn what he once was. For Möhler these truths of revelation are to be found enshrined in the teaching of the Council of Trent.[20]

Möhler notes that the teachings of Trent are meant to bear on "the whole

---

[19]*S*, pp. 55ff.

[20]*S*, Sec. 1, pp. 55-63. A full listing of the texts discussed by Möhler is to be found in Geiselmann's critical apparatus, *S, II*, pp. 18-102.

spiritual as well as corporeal existence of the paradisaic man." Moreover, it was the intention of the fathers of Trent to speak not only of Adam's particular privileges but also of "those gifts which he possessed in common with all men, so far at least as the doctrinal controversies of the sixteenth century required a special explanation on this latter point."[21] Within the limits suggested, therefore, the discussion is to concern, not only Adam, but, in a word, human nature.

As the Catechism of the Council of Trent describes him, the first man may be thought of as follows:

> With respect to the soul, God formed man in his image and likeness and gave him free will; he so regulated man's other movements and desires that they would always obey the rule of reason.

> He fashioned the body in such a manner that, not, indeed, by its own strength, but by a divine gift it would be immortal and impassible.[22]

Simply by reason of his human nature, then, Adam was an image of God, that is, a spiritual being endowed with freedom of choice and capable of knowing and loving God in a manner undisturbed by unruly feelings of desire or lassitude. But Adam also had supernatural gifts, gifts supplementing the powers of his rational soul, far exceeding in worth his "preternatural" gifts of bodily impassibility and immortality. He was—and this was the root of the entirety of his well-being—"constituted," as the Council itself has it, "in justice and holiness."[23]

Constituted in justice and holiness—the fathers of Trent did not describe Adam's condition before the fall more precisely than this. What they meant is clear, namely that Adam was perfectly pleasing to God. Their admittedly sketchy description of original justice was sufficient to meet their concerns: to state clearly that the evil that is in the world does not come from God (in which case the doctrine of God as holy world-creator would be faulted) as well as that the redemption of man is unmerited (in which case it might be overlooked that man is a sinner through his own fault). Further precisions on just how man was at first completely pleasing to God were left to the theologians, that is, they were not made a subject of officially defined doctrine.

It must be kept in mind that when it is said that Adam was completely pleasing to God it is not meant that he simply did nothing against God, but rather that he stood in the most intimate relationship with God. Such a relationship as Adam's, it must be emphasized, one of complete pleasingness before God, is absolutely impossible for unaided human nature. This relationship must be a divine gift; it must be recognized

> that such a relation to God as that of the paradisaic man is no wise to be

[21] *S*, p. 57 (Eng. p. 23).

[22] *S*, pp. 58f., n.n. 1 and 3.

[23] Sess. V, "Decree on Original Sin," can. 1.

attained and upheld by natural powers, that consequently a special condescension of the Almighty is required thereto; in short, that no finite being can exist
in a living moral communion with the Deity, save by the communion of the
self-same holy spirit. This relation of Adam to God, as it exalted him above
human nature and made him participate in that of God, is hence termed . . . a
supernatural gift of divine grace, superadded to the endowments of nature.[24]

Möhler notes that were this extremely important point not clear enough from
the teachings of Trent further clarification might be had from Pius V's and
Gregory XIII's condemnations of the doctrine of Michael Baius, who held that,
even if original justice cannot be strictly considered an element of human nature,
it is still strictly *due* to a creature with that nature.[25] The dogma of the Roman
Church is that this original elevation of Adam was "a special condescension," "a
gift," in short, grace. Even if as elements of his human nature Adam received
reason and freedom from God, complete pleasingness before God could result
only from an additional gracious gift from him. This doctrinal position, Möhler
adds, is the Christian's best bulwark against philosophical pantheism; for when-
ever from a purely philosophical point of view men try to conceptualize the
God-man relationship, they more often than not deify themselves by affirming a
pantheistic likeness of nature between themselves and God.

In their efforts to shed further light on the mystery of original justice,
Möhler continues, some theologians have described the complex of Adam's
preternatural and supernatural gifts as an accidental perfection which maintained
a harmonious relationship between man's sensory and rational powers, and
which was imparted to man at the moment of creation. Although this description is not demonstrably false, it is not as exact as it might be. A better way of
coming to terms with Adam's original situation is to affirm that Adam was
created with an already harmonious nature, and that only after the passage of
some time did God give him grace, only after Adam had in some way been
prepared, and had prepared himself by the (unmeritorious, of course) exercise of
his freedom, for these gifts. This point of view has a number of advantages. What
man is capable of by himself is made more evident. So also is both man's natural
capacity to receive grace as well as the "graciousness" of what grace brings. It is
made clear in addition that the fall is in no sense a result of creation; at the
outset man is seen to be in no misrelation to God, and if such a misrelation

---

[24]*S*, pp. 58f. (Eng., pp. 24f.).

[25]Möhler did not originally consider the papal condemnations of Baius to be dogmati-
cally binding (see *S, II*, pp. 157f.). Döllinger convinced him to change his mind on this point
(see Möhler, *Aktenstücke und Briefe*, pp. 223f.). The letter referred to here is dated 1830;
an intriguing aspect of Möhler's theological development is the role that continued historical
study had in gradually making him an orthodox representative of his own church (although
his "orthodoxy," in Vatican I-II terms, has a Jansenist tinge). Georges Goyau, in his valuable
preface to *Moehler* (sel. texts in Fr. trans.) (Paris, 1903), suggests, pp. 11f., that Möhler was
"le théologien le plus autodidacte des temps modernes."

subsequently arises, it is clear that it comes about solely through man's fault. Similarly it is more evident that man comes to full consciousness of his nature as well as of God's readiness to help him without the introduction of evil into the world. Finally, man's possibilities after the fall, once it has taken place, and the nature of fallen man's return to God are significantly prefigured. No matter how it is described in detail, however, the gist of the Catholic position remains that the grace whereby Adam was made completely pleasing to God cannot in any way be considered constitutive of or due to human nature.

Möhler now takes up the Reformers' position on the original state of man.[26] Luther, he says, never doubted that Adam was originally positively holy and just. He was completely unacquainted with that later doctrine which maintains that Adam found himself, as a figure of all men, in a paradisaic state of indifference or unspecification between good and evil, that for him to come to self-consciousness as man the experience of a fall was necessary. (Möhler does not deny that a trial of Adam was necessary, or that the fall did in fact increase Adam's self-awareness; he, denies only that the fall as such was necessary, that a passage through absurdity is the necessary precondition for the life of reason.) If Luther avoided this error, however, he fell into another.

What Luther did was to revive an earlier, scholastic doctrine to the effect that Adam's righteousness was not a supernatural gift but rather an aspect of man's nature, indeed, a necessary constituent of man's nature. In Luther's words, "Let us rather maintain that righteousness was not a gift which came from without, separate from man's nature, but that it was truly part of his nature, so that it was Adam's nature to love God, to believe God, to know God, etc."[27]

What Luther maintained, in other words, is that the ethico-religious capability of man is, without further qualification, to be named the image of God in man. Luther did not distinguish between the possibility of pleasing God and the actual performance of acts in conformity with the divine will. Simply because Adam had this capability he was religious, pleasing to God. The Catholic theologians, on the other hand, clearly distinguished between the capability and the proper use of it, which last they termed, in distinction to "image," the "likeness" of God. As will soon be evident, this apparently unimportant distinction becomes very important when the question of the nature of original sin arises. Despite Luther's laudable wish to avoid the subtleties of the later scholastics, he fell into a worse error than they did.

In addition to his mistaken conception of the relationship between man's nature and divine grace, Luther had a correspondingly faulty understanding of how grace assists man when human nature passes into actual operation, of, that is to say, the nature of human freedom. Luther, says Möhler, wanted it accepted

---

[26]*S*, Sec. 2, pp. 63-69.

[27]*S*, p. 64. *Lectures on Genesis*, tr. G. V. Schlick, *Luther's Works*, ed. J. Pelikan, I (St. Louis, 1958), 165.

as an article of faith "that man is devoid of freedom, that every (pretended) free action is only apparent, that an irresistible divine necessity rules all things, and that every human act is at bottom only the act of God."[28] In the *De Servo Arbitrio* Luther states that divine causality and foreknowledge quite rule out a real freedom of choice in man:

> It is fundamentally necessary and wholesome for Christians to know that God knows nothing contingently, but that he foresees, purposes, and does all things according to his own immutable, eternal and infallible will. This bombshell knocks "free will" flat, and utterly shatters it.[29]

Moreover, Luther's position was shared by Melanchthon, who in the first edition of his *Loci Theologici* wrote, "Inasmuch as everything that happens happens necessarily, our will has no freedom."[30] It is noteworthy that after a riper experience as a man and a theologian Melanchthon, in the 1535 edition of the *Loci,* withdrew this doctrine. Luther, however, never changed his mind, and it was his position against Erasmus that was confirmed in the *Formula of Concord.*[31]

The teaching of Calvin and his followers on the original state of man is essentially the same as that of the Lutherans.[32] Calvin's position differs superficially from theirs in that he affirms freedom to be a necessary attribute of human nature; the freedom in question, however—and here he rejoins the Lutherans—is not a true freedom of choice but only freedom from external coercion. Even if certain creatures act spontaneously, therefore, what they do is no less necessary, for God's will governs absolutely everything; even the fall necessarily occurs. Although it is true that Calvin emphasized the absolute universality of divine causality in order to stimulate Christians to trust in God, it must nevertheless be said that Calvin's manner of emphasizing this makes it appear as if God is the cause, not only of good, but of evil as well, and what is most abhorrent, of moral evil.

But if God is not the cause of moral evil, how, in general, does moral evil arise?[33] In the sixteenth century, Möhler notes, the question of the origin of moral evil was a hotly debated one. No doctrine of the Reformers evoked a sharper response from their Catholic critics than their conception of the relationship between God and evil; the errors of the Reformers were what brought about the great subsequent Catholic emphasis on man's freedom of choice. If man is

---

[28] *S,* p. 67 (Eng., pp. 29f.).

[29] *S,* p. 67. Eng. tr. by J. I. Packer and O. R. Johnson, *The Bondage of the Will* (Edinburgh, 1957), Chap. II, sec. 4, p. 80; compare Chap. V, sec. 8, pp. 216-18.

[30] *S,* p. 68, nn. 6-7.

[31] *S,* p. 68.

[32] *S,* Sec. 3, pp. 69-74.

[33] *S,* Sec. 4, pp. 74-85.

free, the responsibility for moral evil falls squarely on his shoulders; if not, then God must be less than good, must be the cause of evil.

That God is indeed the cause of moral evil is precisely what Melanchthon taught in his commentary on Romans of 1523: "For it is established that God does not merely permit all things, but actually [*potenter*] brings them about, in such a manner, that is, that the treason of Judas is just as much his own proper work as the vocation of Paul."[34] It is true, of course, that this passage was suppressed in later editions of this work. Nevertheless, the attempt by Chemnitz to excuse Melanchthon's earlier lapse on the grounds that Catholic overemphasis on freedom had obscured the question is abruptly dismissed by Möhler.[35] The question is an old one, and Melanchthon should have known better. It is clear, at any rate, that Melanchthon was simply prefiguring what Luther would teach in the *De Servo Arbitrio.*

In the Catholic view God is not, of course, the author of evil, and in stating this view the fathers of Trent appear to have had Melanchthon in mind:

> If anyone says that it is not in man's power to make his ways evil, but that the works that are evil as well as those that are good God produces, not permissively only but also *proprie et per se,* so that the treason of Judas is no less His own proper work than the vocation of St. Paul, let him be anathema.[36]

As already noted, however, Melanchthon thought the better of this position. In the Augsburg Confession he wrote:

> It is taught among us that although almighty God has created and still preserves nature, yet sin is caused in all wicked men and despisers of God by the perverted will. This is the will of the devil and of all ungodly men; as soon as God withdraws his support, the will turns away from God to evil. It is as Christ says in John 8:44, "When the devil lies, he speaks according to his own nature."[37]

The Solid Declaration repeats this view: "It is also a clearly established truth . . . that God is not the creator, author, or cause of sin. Through Satan's scheme, 'by one man sin (which is the work of the devil) entered into the world.'"[38] Man, not God, is the author of human moral evil.

The Swiss Reformers, on the other hand, took a more consistent, but also a

---

[34]*S,* p. 75.

[35]*S,* pp. 74f., n. 1.

[36]*S,* p. 76 (*Canons and Decrees of the Council of Trent,* tr. H. J. Schroeder (St. Louis, 1941), p. 43. (Sess. V, "Decree on Justification," can. 6.)

[37]*Ibid.* (See *Die Bekenntnisschriften der evangelisch-lutherischen Kirche* [Göttingen, 1959⁴], p. 75. Hereafter abbreviated *BK.* English translation: *The Book of Concord: The Confessions of the Evangelical-Lutheran Church,* tr. Theodore G. Tappert *et al.* [Philadelphia, 1959], pp. 40f.)

[38]*Ibid.* (*BK,* p. 847; Eng., p. 510).

much more grievous stand. Zwingli wrote that God moves, indeed, drives man to sin; and Calvin and Beza followed his lead. Their assertion that God's universal purpose in effect sanctifies the means used to realize it, that is, his causing men to do evil, is not, according to Möhler, a satisfactory response. It is unsatisfactory because it creates a dilemma in which either the divine holiness or the divinely grounded objectivity of the moral law must be denied. What the Swiss did, therefore, was to develop more fully the contradiction in the original Lutheran position. If man, as the image of God, is not thought of as being by nature reasonable and free, God must be thought to be the author of moral evil. If there is no freedom of choice for men, one can conclude only that absolutely everything is immediately subject to divine necessitation.

Original Sin

In Chapter II of Book I Möhler takes up the doctrine of original sin. He begins his discussion by pointing out that, as already intimated, by reason of their conception of Adam's nature, particularly his freedom before the fall, the Protestants cannot possibly have a coherent doctrine of original sin.[39]

> It is one of the most remarkable phenomena in the history of the religious controversies of the last three centuries that the Reformers, according to whose principles Adam in his fall only succumbed under a sentence of irresistible necessity pronounced upon him, should have represented the deity as kindling into so fearful a wrath and inflicting so frightful a chastisement for this *act* of the first man, which, according to their own views, should be called rather his pure misfortune. It is no easy task to explain how ideas so unconnected should have been associated in one and the same head.[40]

How could Adam deserve such a punishment, if he only did what he had to do, what he could not, in the face of complete divine necessitation, avoid? How could the Swiss Reformers follow so blindly in the footsteps of Luther and Melanchthon, a circumstance which makes it possible to speak of a single "Protestant" position? Surely, says Möhler, this Protestant position that would punish Adam for what he could not avoid is "ohne Sinn und Verstand": Protestantism is fundamentally absurd.[41]

It becomes apparent now why Möhler chose the doctrines of the state of Adam before the fall and of the origin of evil to begin his comparison of Catholic and Protestant "anthropology." Thus to follow the history of the race step by step, he said, was the simplest manner of accomplishing his purpose. It is

[39]*S*, Sec. 5, pp. 86-99. Möhler's principal emendation of his text occurs in this section; see *S, II*, pp. 164-81.

[40]*S*, p. 86 (Eng., p. 43).

[41]*S*, p. 45. This off-hand remark of Möhler becomes the battle-cry of Baur's replies.

clear now that this sought-for simplicity has not merely to do with the reader's ease of comprehension. Rather, what is at stake here is the structure of Möhler's understanding of "Protestant" thought, if not theology generally. What Möhler is saying is that when treating of Protestantism it is simplest to begin with the doctrines of original justice and original evil because it was precisely here that Protestants made and continue to make their basic error. Whereas the Reformers were primarily concerned with justification, and whereas many Protestants still believe this doctrine to be the center of their faith, the real basis of Protestantism as a system of thought is its understanding of human nature in its first unspoiled moments. Möhler's discussion of the history of the human race from its first moments onward is meant to have, not only a quasi-chronological, but also a strictly logical, systematic simplicity.

Compared with the Protestant doctrine of original sin, the Catholic doctrine is simple and moderate.[42] Adam's disobedience weakened him in body and soul. After Adam's sin neither he nor his progeny could so act as to be completely pleasing to God. They were such that they could return to divine favor only through the merits of Christ, the sole mediator between God and man. Still, man was not so wounded in the fall that he lost his reason and his freedom of choice, even if these powers became somewhat weakened. Man is still the image of God, then, even if he does not always continue in the likeness of God. It is thus excessive to say that prior to justification, all man's acts are sins.

It is evident that the fathers of Trent understood as their task (in accordance with the instructions they received from the pope) simply to state, with reference to Protestantism, what original sin is not, not to put forward a positive position on the subject. To go beyond what was decided upon at Trent, Möhler concedes, is a very difficult task, and Catholic attempts at formulating an exact definition of what original sin is and how it passes from Adam to his progeny have given rise to much misunderstanding. Still, says Möhler, to affirm that the teaching of the scholastics, such as Bonaventure and Thomas, is tainted with Pelagianism is a wholly mistaken venture. It was precisely their acute sense of the weakened state of man's mind and will, as well as of man's lack of full rational control over his sense appetites, that made it so difficult for them to discuss the transmission of original sin. A materialistic explanation of that transmission would be absurd, whereas it is difficult to imagine how the human soul could emerge in a weakened condition from the hands of its Creator. Despite the difficulties of the problem, however, the great scholastic theologians never hinted, in Pelagian fashion, that this problem was only an apparent one.

As for the Lutherans, a clear statement of their doctrine on original sin is to be found in the Apology of the Augsburg Confession: it is asserted "that in those who are born according to the flesh we deny the existence not only of actual fear and trust in God but also of the possibility and gift to produce it."[43]

---

[42]*S*, pp. 87-99.

[43]*S*, p. 100, n. 3 (*BK*, p. 146; Eng., p. 101). For the Lutheran doctrine of original sin as a whole see *S*, Sec. 6, pp. 99-115.

The doctrine put forward here is simply that of Luther himself, who in his commentary on Genesis teaches that "original righteousness belonged to the nature of man; if it was lost by sin, the natural endowment of man did not, as the scholastics ravingly assert, remain whole."[44] Yet, it might be asked, to what extent did the natural in man not remain whole? It is now for the first time apparent, Möhler notes, with what serious consequences the Lutheran doctrine of the original state of man is attended. If all that Adam had before the fall belonged to his nature as man, and if he now has less in the way of capabilities, the only conclusion that one can draw is that the fall somehow altered and diminished human nature in Adam. It is no longer a case, as with the Catholic position, primarily of Adam's losing certain supernatural helps toward living a harmonious life, but rather, fundamentally, of Adam's becoming radically different from what he was before, of his being *essentially* changed.

When, Möhler continues, the opinion of Valentin Strigel, more moderate than that of Luther, occasioned the synergist controversy, the Lutheran position was reaffirmed and clarified in the Formula of Concord: "Prior to his conversion man is dead in sin (Eph. 2:5); hence there can be in him no power to do something good in divine matters, and he cannot have a mode of acting in divine matters."[45] It is clear, notes Möhler, that "by the declaration of the Formula of Concord . . . it was not thereby intended to hold fallen man for an irrational creature."[46] The case is rather that the Formula of Concord "to that faculty of the human mind which *it* terms reason . . . assigns merely the finite world as the sphere or activity" and asserts that "Adam . . . and all his descendents, considered merely as such, have no longer preserved any spiritual aptitude for God . . . ."[47]

That the Lutherans maintain that man has not the capability of attaining God by reason, and yet has reason, is, for Möhler, simply incoherent. Rationality is one whole, as is the essence of man itself; how can man lose a part of that organic whole?

> It is indeed absolutely inconceivable how out of the organism of the human mind a link could be plucked out and destroyed; how any faculty of a simple essence, uncompounded of parts, whose faculties science only separates and distinguishes (for they in themselves are one in all and all in one), should be loosed from the others and be annihilated; but we have not yet done with the impenetrable obscurity of the Lutheran theory of original sin.[48]

[44]*S*, p. 100, n. 4. *WA* XLII, col. 125; compare *Luther's Works, ibid.*, p. 166.

[45]*S*, p. 102, n. 8 (*BK*, p. 896; Eng., p. 533).

[46]*S*, p. 103 (Eng., p. 55).

[47]*S*, pp. 103f. (Eng., pp. 55f.).

[48]*S*, pp. 106f. (Eng., p. 57).

By no means! Luther, says Möhler, attempts to reason from his conception of original sin to the character of original justice, namely, that original justice must be the faculty to love and discern God. But then "original sin must in his opinion be THE FACULTY not to love God and not to discern Him . . . !"[49]

Original sin, therefore, considered as an integral part of fallen man's nature, must be something *positive,* something evil that really exists in its own right and is not merely the lack of something that should be present. According to a group of Luther's formulas assembled by Quenstedt, "the nature of man is sin, it is the essence of man to be sin, after the fall the nature of man is altered, that which is born of father and mother is itself original sin, man is sin itself,"[50] and so forth. Quite in harmony with this view is that of the Solid Declaration:

> original sin . . . replaces the lost image of God in man with a deep, wicked, abominable, bottomless, inscrutable, and inexpressible corruption of his entire nature in all its powers, especially of the highest and foremost powers of the soul in mind, heart and will.[51]

From his parents fallen man receives "an inborn wicked stamp, an interior uncleanness of the heart and evil desires and inclinations."[52]

How could such a doctrine ever come to be formulated? The Lutheran doctrine of original sin, as Möhler sees it, is clearly the result of feelings that are in themselves praiseworthy, a deep sense of human misery and sinfulness and an ardent desire for redemption. What apparently happened, however, was that these feelings were not accompanied by the necessary intellectual self-criticism. The conception of sinful man that arose from these unanalyzed feelings, nonetheless, leads one to think that God, in so altering man's very essence, has dealt with his creature in a purely mechanical manner. With man's powers regarding spiritual things gone, actually it is no longer possible for man to sin, at least not until the coming of Christ, and all reason for the long delay of his coming is exploded. All moral evil is, in fact, transmuted into physical evil, for man is no longer thought to be a responsible being. Man, remarks Möhler, "may rave—he may be furious—he may destroy, but his mode of acting cannot be considered other than that of a savage beast."[53]

An additional difficulty arising from the Lutheran doctrine is that of accounting for the knowledge of and desire for God that history demonstrates to have been present in all periods and cultures.[54] It is no Pelagian denial of man's true state after the fall, but rather proof of a greater sensitivity to it, to take

[49]*S,* pp. 106f. (Eng., p. 58).

[50]*S,* p. 108, n. 18.

[51]*S,* p. 109, n. 20 (*BK,* p. 848; Eng., p. 510).

[52]*S,* p. 110, n. 20 (*BK* and Eng., *ibid.*).

[53]*S,* pp. 112f. (Eng., p. 62).

[54]*S,* Sec. 7, pp. 115-23.

seriously the mixture of superstition and desire for redemption that is to be found, for example, in the religions of China and India. The fact that these religions do not themselves justify does not take from the fact that they are available for the serious observation of anyone who cares to familiarize himself with them. To be consistent, Lutherans must say with Melanchthon: "Granted that there was in Socrates a certain constancy, in Xenocrates chastity, in Zeno temperance, ... these qualities must not be regarded as real virtues, but as vices,"[55] even though the Solid Declaration, wholly illogically, would affirm that human reason still has "a dim spark of the knowledge that there is a God."[56] In any case, if man does not now and since the fall never did possess ethical freedom, the history of the race is rendered barren and meaningless as a properly human progress. The reader can now begin to see, notes Möhler, what was meant when it was said that, depending on whether one's point of view is Catholic or Protestant, all history looks different.

Calvin, as Möhler understands him, appears to be rather more reasonable, although this reasonableness is purchased at the price of unclarity.[57] Calvin states that the image of God in man is destroyed; yet he also maintains that

> Even though we grant that God's image was not totally annihilated and destroyed in him, yet it was so corrupted that whatever remains is frightful deformity. ... Now God's image is the perfect excellence of human nature which shone in Adam before his defection, but was subsequently so vitiated and almost blotted out that nothing remains after the ruin except what is confused, mutilated, and disease-ridden.[58]

Calvin, similarly, notes that fallen man can indeed know something of God—but only in vain. The good to be found in non-Christians receives scant recognition. What seems to be the case for Calvin is that though man does have sufficient reason and will to distinguish him from beasts, it is still incorrect to say that "man has preserved out of his unhappy catastrophe any moral and religious *powers whatever.*"[59] As for Zwingli, Möhler notes briefly that his wish to treat original sin as an aspect of human nature leads him, like the Lutherans, to transmute moral into physical evil; nonetheless, this position coheres perfectly with Zwingli's conception of universal divine causality, in which properly *moral* evil cannot occur.

In summary, Möhler finds that because Protestants exalt man before the fall they must debase him after it: if it was man's *nature* to be wholly pleasing

---

[55]*S*, p. 118, n. 3.

[56]*S*, p. 117, n. 1 (*BK*, p. 874; Eng., p. 521).

[57]*S*, Sec. 8, pp. 124-32.

[58]*Institutes of the Christian Religion,* Bk. I, Chap. 15, Sec. 4., tr. F. L. Battles, I (Philadelphia, 1960), 189.

[59]*S*, Sec. 9, pp. 133-35.

to God before the fall, one can only conclude that after it man has slipped toward bestiality. But then man is no longer man, no longer free and responsible. And God, therefore, must be the author of evil. Compared with the balance of Catholicism, Protestantism is indeed "ohne Sinn und Verstand"! Such, albeit with regret, is the conclusion that the careful symbolical theologian must draw.

In Chapter III of the *Symbolik* Möhler discusses justification, faith, and good works, noting that Catholic and Protestant views on these topics are simply the necessary result of the positions taken on original sin and original justice. Though it is true that, in terms of sixteenth-century history, justification was the central issue of the Reformation, the fact remains that, from a *systematic* point of view, theories of justification are simply corollaries of options taken in theological anthropology.[60] The historical immediacy of *my* justification is comprehensible only in terms of my inheritance and prospects as a son of Adam. At any rate, Möhler's Chapter III is simply the application of theses established in Chapters I and II, indeed, of a fundamental thesis announced in his preface to the *Symbolik:* whereas for the last fifty years Catholics have been called upon to defend only the divine elements in Christianity, they are now required to uphold its *human* elements in the Christian religion. The essentially Pelagian Enlightenment is over and done with; now, faced with an unholy alliance of resuscitated Protestant orthodoxy and pantheistic idealism, centrist Catholicism must defend man's ability to cooperate in his own salvation.[61]

Möhler's theological anthropology bears constant witness to this synergistic dignity of man. Man's estate is so noble that, even though man is fallen, man's acts can yet become also God's acts. The incarnation of God in Christ is paradigmatic for the divine-human sacramentality of Christ's church.[62] When, in Chapter IV, Möhler discusses the Catholic sacraments, he stresses that

> The Church . . . is the living figure of Christ, manifesting himself and working through all ages, whose atoning and redeeming acts it in consequence eternally repeats and uninterruptedly continues . . . . He is eternally living in his Church, and in the sacrament of the altar he has manifested this in a sensible manner to creatures endowed with sense.[63]

The eucharist is, of course, the center of Catholic incarnationalism, and thus the Catholic understanding of the eucharist, of the sacrifice of the Mass, is the key to understanding what is at once the incarnation of the divine and the divinization of the human:

> When we wish to express ourselves accurately, the sacrifice of Christ on the

---

[60]*S*, p. 136 (Eng., pp. 83f.).

[61]*S*, p. 12.

[62]*S*, pp. 387f.

[63]*S*, pp. 353f. (Eng., p. 231).

cross is put only as a part for an organic whole. For his whole life on earth—his
ministry and his sufferings, as well as his perpetual condescension to our
infirmity in the Eucharist—constitute one great sacrificial act, one mighty
action undertaken out of love for us and expiatory of our sins, consisting,
indeed, of various individual parts, yet so that none by itself is strictly speaking the sacrifice. In each particular part the whole recurs, yet without these
parts the whole cannot be conceived.[64]

How great the dignity of Catholic man! What Christ did on the cross and
what *we* can do form *one organic whole.* Möhler's theology of the church, in
Chapter V, complements his theology of the Mass. Word and Spirit come
together from the Father. Those who, outwardly, truly celebrate the Mass have
inwardly received the Spirit; and "the Divine Spirit, to which are intrusted the
guidance and vivification of the Church, becomes in its union with the human
spirit in the Church a peculiarly Christian tact, a deep sure-guiding feeling,
which,. as it abides in truth, leads into all truth."[65] The Catholic hierarchy,
therefore, are not an alien authority, but simply the spokesmen, indeed, the
symbols, of the one faith of all who have received, outwardly, the scriptural and
sacramental Word, and, inwardly, the divine Spirit. Hierarchy and faithful are
together possessors of this "peculiarly Christian tact," together exemplars of the
divine spirit "in its union with the human spirit."[66] Protestantism, however,
fails to grasp the implications of the union of God and man in Christ, precisely
because of its low estimate of post-Adamic man. In short, it misrepresents both
Christ and the Christian.

[64]*S,* pp. 357-59 (Eng., p. 232). Many of Möhler's ideas about the church—particularly
regarding *living tradition,* expressed both in the eucharist and in doctrinal development—
have passed into Roman Catholic magisterial teaching; see P. Riga, "The Ecclesiology of J.
A. Möhler," *Theological Studies,* XXII (1961), 586f.

[65]*S,* p. 413 (Eng., p. 271).

[66]*S,* Sec. 43, pp. 448-56. Möhler, however, was writing *before* Vatican I. Thus, he says,
"it is well known that, partly in consequence of the revolutions of time and of disorders in
the Church, partly through the internal development of opposite ideas, two systems became
prevalent [in church polity], the episcopal system and the papal system, the latter whereof,
without questioning the divine institution of bishops, exalted more particularly the central
power, while the former, without denying the divine establishment of the primacy, sought
to draw authority more particularly toward the circumference." These two points of view,
adds Möhler, "constituted an opposition very beneficial to ecclesiastical life, so that by their
counteraction the peculiar free development of the several parts was, on the one hand,
preserved, and the union of these in one living, indivisible whole was, on the other, maintained" (*S,* pp. 453f.; Eng., pp. 301f.). Current Roman Catholic emphasis on "collegiality"
would seem in some measure to vindicate Möhler's (and his friend Döllinger's) views—and at
least incipiently to reverse the nineteenth-century "capture" of Roman Catholicism by a
curialist (as opposed to a "Gallican" or German-Romantic) conception of church polity.
Further discussion of Möhler's understanding of justification, sacraments, and the church
may be found in *MBC,* Chap. III, pp. 92-135.

Conclusion: General Comparison of Catholicism and Protestantism

The first basic problem with Protestantism is that it misunderstands the reason for the incarnation. More precisely, it tends to separate the offices of the Redeemer. As Luther himself put it, the Word of God came on earth, not to teach the law, but to redeem us from sin; if Christ did in fact teach, his teaching was no more central to his mission than his curing the sick.[67] The task of Luther's Christ was to fulfill the law, and to remove it, not as the foolish scholastics taught, to teach mankind a new law, even a law of love. The gospel which Christ brings is in no sense law; law and gospel are forever to be distinguished.

But, replies Möhler, the various elements of the life and work of Christ cannot be so summarily distinguished; rather

> the life of the Saviour constitutes in every relation an organic unity; and everything in him, his sufferings and his works, his doctrines, his conduct, his death on the cross, were in a like degree calculated for our redemption. It is the merits of the entire, undivided God-man, the Son of God, whereby we are won again to God. His three offices, the prophetic, the high-priestly, the royal, are alike necessary; take one away, and the remaining immediately appear as unintelligible, as devoid of consistency. Thus, by the advent of the Son of God into the world there were proffered to men, not by accident, but by *necessity* at once the highest degree of religious and ethical knowledge, the ideal of a life agreeable to God, forgiveness of sins, and a sanctifying power; and as in the one life of the Saviour we find all these united so they must in like manner be adopted by us.[68]

If the teaching and other offices of Christ cannot be separated, however, it must still be asked how it is possible for Christ both to originate the highest ethical demands and yet to preach the forgiveness of sins. The unifying element, replies Möhler,

> is the sanctifying power which emanates from living union with Christ, the *gratuitous grace* of holy love which, in justification, he pours out upon his followers. In this grace all law is abolished, because no outward claim is enforced; and, at the same time, the law is confirmed, because love is the fulfilment of the law: in love law and grace are become one. This is the deep sense of the Catholic dogma of justification, according to which forgiveness of sins and sanctification are one and the same, according to which justification consists in the reign of love in the soul.[69]

The upshot of all this is that Catholicism is able to affirm a unity of religion

---

[67]*S*, p. 267. For the comparison, see *S*, Secs. 24-27, pp. 266-302. Möhler's general remarks appear at the end of his discussion of justification (Chap. III), not (as with Baur) at the end of his whole treatment of the controverted issues.

[68]*S*, p. 277 (Eng., p. 178).

[69]*S*, p. 278 (Eng., p. 179).

and morality, whereas Protestantism is not:

> This so decided and unreconciled opposition between gospel and law leads to a
> total degradation of the latter, so that all the differences between Catholicism
> and Protestantism in the article of justification may shortly be reduced to this,
> namely, that the Catholic Church considers religion and morality as inwardly
> one and the same, while the Protestant Church represents the two as essential-
> ly distinct—the former as having an eternal, the latter a temporal value.[70]

In this separation of the foundation of the God-man relationship from man's
subsequent conduct, in this degradation of morality, of course, lie the roots of
antinomianism; in opposing the "fanatics" Luther was acting rightly but illogically. He was similarly illogical in asserting that for offenses against this temporal
law man deserves eternal punishment. He was yet again illogical in degrading the
law that is presumably the very will of God to which grace is meant to reconcile
us. Only love, rooted in human freedom, is the unity of religion and morality.

The second basic problem with Protestantism, the more fundamental of the
two, is its Christian anthropology, which denies man's freedom. What seems,
from a speculative point of view, to lie at the root of Protestant doctrine is the
thought that finitude is necessarily evil: "The sense of sin cannot be effaced
from all finite consciousness; . . . it constantly accompanies and tortures man,
because evil is inseparable from him as a limited being; to this he is
predestined."[71] It must immediately be added, of course, that this is not the
doctrine of the Reformers in so many words. What it is is the logical carrying out
of what they taught—and it may also be added that if they had seen the consequences of their doctrines they would not have taught them.[72] What happened
in the case of Luther, for example, is that his feelings led him astray, led him to
misconceive the nature of human freedom:

> The principle of freedom Luther did not apprehend; since in it he abhorred
> the destruction of all deeper religious feeling and true humility, viewing in it
> an encroachment on the rights of the Divine Majesty, nay, the self-deification
> of man. To be free and to be God was, in his opinion, synonymous.[73]

Luther's uncritical religiosity led him to teach doctrines the consequences of
which he doubtless would have rejected, doctrines that amount not only to a
degradation of morality, but, what is far worse, to a degradation of both man
himself, and worse still, of his Creator. The root of Luther's error was that he
lumped together all the meanings of freedom, in particular, the perfect freedom
of untrammeled power and the simple freedom of choice, which latter is another

[70]*S*, p. 279 (Eng., p. 180).

[71]*S*, p. 287 (Eng., p. 186).

[72]*S*, pp. 287f.

[73]*S*, p. 290 (Eng., p. 188).

thing altogether. As Möhler observes, "The freedom of election is for man the necessary condition to a higher freedom, but not the same."[74] That man *can* choose between alternatives does not mean that man *does* choose the right; and, of course, it cannot possibly mean that, no matter how man uses his freedom, man, by happening to be endowed with freedom of choice, becomes literally divine. With freedom of choice gone, however, Protestantism cannot explain the origin of moral evil in a satisfactory manner. God, concludes Protestantism, is the author of evil.

In following the path that it did, Protestantism was not so original as might at first be thought.[75] Möhler's final blow at Protestantism takes the following form:

> Had Luther felt, in a higher degree than we can discover in him, the want of a more general completion and more consistent development of his views, he would most certainly have embraced the opinion of a merely righteous Demiurgos, as asserted by the Gnostics; laid claim to their heretical antino-mianism in behalf of the Pneumatici; and, like Marcion, have separated the Old from the New Testament. Marcion, too, was unable to reconcile law and grace, the all-good, merciful God, with the God who imposes moral precepts and who chastises . . . .[76]

Möhler develops his comparison of Protestantism with Gnosticism along four lines. Both were born of a feeling of misery in this present life. Both, nonetheless, felt no responsibility for their misery: the real problem lay with human nature itself. Both groups considered themselves the elect—in the case of the Protestants, through the doctrine of election to justification by faith. Finally, both separated the Old and New Testaments. The Protestants, of course, are not Gnostics—but were they more self-conscious they surely would be.

Gnosticism as understood by Möhler is a practical state of mind, a way of dealing with the miseries of temporal existence.[77] Gnosticism made speculative, however, is *pantheism,* a position to which—entirely logically—Zwingli pushed Luther's more pedestrian opinions. The ultimate meaning of the Reformation and its consequences as elements in the history of ideas is that the Reformation continued and made more manifest, in a modified form, the pantheism of the Middle Ages:

> Another doctrine to which Protestantism bears undeniable relationship is ideal

[74]*Ibid.*

[75]See especially *S,* Sec. 27, pp. 292-302.

[76]*S,* pp. 282f. (Eng., p. 182).

[77]See Möhler, "Versuch über den Ursprung des Gnostizismus," *Gesammelte Schriften und Aufsätze,* ed. I. Döllinger (Regensburg, 1839-40; reprinted, Frankfurt a/M, 1971), I, 403-35. In this article of 1831 Möhler holds that Gnosticism was primarily a practical stance taken only when people tried to provide a theoretical justification for their excessive feelings did they fall into theoretical heresy.

Pantheism, whose adherents, through the whole course of the middle age, were
arrayed against the Church in no less violent opposition than that which she
encountered from the Gnostico-Manichean Dualists.[78]

Zwingli, says Möhler, continued in the line of Amalric of Chartres and David of
Dinant; he put forth essentially the same doctrine as the various radical apocaly-
ptic groups, such as the Lollards and the Brethren of the Free Spirit. Zwingli
followed in their footsteps, for

> they held the doctrine of the One and All of things—of the absolute necessity
> of everything which occurs—and, consequently, of evil in the creation, of the
> want of free-will in man, and yet of the utmost latitude of freedom, which he
> can enforce against the dictates of the moral law—of the certainty of
> salvation—that is to say, the return to the deity, or absorption in His bosom,
> which, indeed, forms a necessary part of Pantheism and of every doctrine that
> ascribes a divine essence to man.[79]

Zwingli, moreover, continued the teaching of Wyclif, who "ascribed ... evil to
God and, with the denial of freedom of election in man, admitted in his system
an absolute predestination."[80] If Zwingli was rather more clairvoyant—not, that
is, about his predecessors, but about the logical virtualities of his position—it must
remain that Luther was the ultimate villain: "Zwingli ... only reduces to its first
principles Luther's doctrine of the servitude of the will."[81]

In both its formal and material principles, therefore, Protestantism stands
revealed as radically opposed to the basic principles of both reason and the
gospel. If only Protestants could see themselves as they are! It is the final
absurdity of Protestantism either not to be able to recognize its absurdity or else
to recognize its true identity and thereby cease to be Christian:

> We have often wondered at the so-called orthodox Protestant theologians of
> our days when they opposed modern theological and philosophical systems
> which more consistently carried out the principles of the Reformers, so little
> did Protestant orthodoxy understand itself! With all his deviations on particu-
> lar points, Schleiermacher is, in my opinion, the only genuine disciple of the
> Reformers.[82]

---

[78]S, p. 297 (Eng., p. 193).

[79]S, pp. 297f. (Eng., p. 193).

[80]S, p. 298 (Eng., p. 193).

[81]S, p. 301 (Eng., p. 196).

[82]S, pp. 301f. (Eng., p. 196).

CHAPTER III

Baur's Gegensatz

The arrangement of Baur's *Der Gegensatz des Katholicismus und Protestantismus* is roughly parallel to that of Book I of Möhler's *Symbolik*. The following examination of Baur's argument can thus take the same shape as Chapter II of the present study—a consideration, first, of symbolics; then of original justice, original sin, and freedom, and then of the more general, fundamental differences between Catholicism and Protestantism.

The Nature of Symbolics

Even if symbolics has the same subject matter as inter-confessional polemics, Baur begins, it has a decidedly different point of view.[1] In opposition to the polemics of earlier eras Baur defines the role of symbolics as follows:

> Its purpose is not merely to deny and to combat, not merely to tear down and to destroy; it treats the doctrinal idea of an adversary not merely as an aggregate of propositions, the refutation of which is simply a matter to be accomplished by extracting them, as single unconnected parts, from a whole that has been broken into pieces. Symbolics, rather, seeks to reconstruct the two opposed doctrinal concepts as systems by grasping each in the unity of its principle, for at the root of each system lies a primary determination of the religious consciousness that bears in itself its own well grounded claim to truth.[2]

Baur and Möhler are in agreement, then, that the second quarter of the nineteenth century is high time to leave off polemics and to begin treating confessional differences scientifically. They are similarly agreed that the scientific treatment of the various doctrinal positions put forward by each side in inter-confessional discussion consists precisely in seeing as a system the totality of what each side has to say. After this point, however, Möhler and Baur part company.

Möhler, it will be remembered, noted that the personal insight of the symbolist tends, *per accidens,* to give his study a polemical character. This personal element does not militate against scientific methodology; on the contrary, it is the very basis of scientific symbolical methodology, for without this personal insight religious data cannot be grasped in an organic, systematic

---

[1]G^2, pp. 1-24.
[2]G^1, p. 3; G^2, p. 3.

manner. Möhler, apparently, was thinking of two rather different tasks in, or levels of, systematic symbolics. First, there is the necessity of seeing a given body of confessional data correctly and as a whole; Möhler and Baur agree on this point. Secondly, however, Möhler states that the personal insight just mentioned will enable the symbolist to grasp the conformity, or want of it, of a given confessional system with the basic truths of Christian philosophy and the gospel. Baur's conception of this second task or level of systematic inquiry is somewhat different.

The role of symbolics as Baur sees it is to grasp the wholeness of systems at the root of each of which "lies a primary determination of the religious consciousness that bears in itself its own well grounded claim to truth." Instead of comparing each system with the basic truths of philosophy or revelation, presumably known independently of these systems, the symbolical theologian is rather to regard each system as the true cognitive reflex of a consciousness that truly and legitimately exists. Baur continues—

> In this respect, what most radically distinguishes symbolics from the old polemics is the scientific handling of its object; symbolics can grasp the doctrinal concepts of the churches only as organically inter-related systems, each of which is determined by its own proper principle; but it is thus self-evident that doctrinal concepts which stand over against each other as do the Catholic and the Protestant ought not be set in opposition simply as truth and error, for in general science has also the task of recognizing in the moments of differentiation the unity of the concept.[3]

The only way, then, of avoiding a fall back into the old polemical *genre* is to admit at the outset that both confessions are legitimately to be seen as moments, that is, as legitimate expressions, of *the* "idea," or of ultimate truth; the right to exist is not to be denied one confession because of what the other asserts. Plainly enough, both already do exist! Nevertheless, adds Baur, it is much easier for Protestants, whose churches make no claim to absolute authority, to follow out this methodology; in fact, it is doubtful whether anyone who adheres fully to Roman Catholicism, whose personal insight has been formed in the Catholic manner, can ever be a scientific symbolical theologian.

It is along these lines that Baur finds the introduction of Möhler's *Symbolik* not only disappointing but deceptive. Only a few pages after Möhler defines symbolics as the "scientific presentation" of the sixteenth-century confessions, he demolishes the confessional character of Protestantism. Protestantism, he says, is only the apotheosis of Luther's ego, and its doctrines cannot be taken in isolation from their source, Luther's subjective feelings. Now, argues Baur, it is plain that Möhler is simply begging the question. Möhler, in refusing to Protes-

---

[3]*Ibid. G*[1], however, reads, ". . . for science, in its higher meaning, leads in general to oppositions of which the unity, though surmised, cannot be presented in a definite concept." Baur's emendation of his text suggests a growing confidence in Hegelian reason as opposed to the intuitive feeling of Schleiermacher.

tantism a claim to truth equal to that of Catholicism, has turned from symbolics back to polemics. On his own principles, with what right can Möhler reduce Protestantism to mere subjectivity? Has he not instead taken for granted what he should be proving and merely set up a straw adversary? Baur feels entitled to conclude that Möhler's claim to scientific objectivity is nothing but an empty show.[4] Möhler's characterization of Protestantism does not cohere with his own presentation of the origin of Protestantism; what Möhler chooses to emphasize is that what occasioned the Reformation was the evil conduct of pre-Reformation *individuals,* and not the essence of Catholicism. In so doing he weakens his position still further, since all that seems to be left of the religious controversy of the sixteenth century is a web of conflicting individualities. Baur asks, "How can one say that an immoderate and fantastic egoism manifested itself in Luther's life and work, if Luther's fight was directed only against such forms of ecclesiastical life as had no other ruling principle than egoism?"[5] It is, to say the least, confusing to assert both that Protestantism is Luther's individuality writ large as well as that Luther began his reforming activity because he confused the sinful individuality of Catholics with Catholicism itself. Luther either dealt in essentials or he did not. But if he did, then his spiritual progeny ought fairly be considered to be doing the same. Needless to say, the fathers of Trent thought that Protestantism threatened the essentials of their position. If the Reformers failed to distinguish the fortuitous from the essential, so, one must argue, did the fathers of Trent! And so, finally, did the author of the *Symbolik*!

There is yet another difficulty in the assertion that Protestantism is absolute subjectivity and error and Catholicism absolute objectivity and truth.[6] The problem lies in what most people understand by the term *subjectivity*:

> Every subjectivity, which has its basis only in itself, must necessarily fall apart as soon as the historical individual who is its bearer has passed out of the circle of his life and work. Only the objective truth has its continuing basis in itself.[7]

The point Baur is making is of course that, strictly speaking, Luther's subjectivity begins and ends with Luther. On the other hand, if Luther can be placed in any sort of historical continuum, then Möhler's understanding of his work is faulty. And, of course, Luther can. Even the Catholics customarily speak of his "forerunners," men such as Wyclif, Hus, and the Waldensians, in general, men whom the Protestants are wont to number in their *catalogus testium veritatis.* To the extent that all these men were objecting to evils in the church, say the Catholics, their work was objective and good; even on the customary principles

---

[4] G^2, p. 14; lacking in G^1. Passages referred to from this note to n. 23 are lacking in G^1.

[5] G^2, pp. 20f.

[6] G^2, pp. 25-59.

[7] G^2, p. 26.

of Catholicism, therefore, Protestantism cannot be absolute falsehood. Even if Catholics cannot admit the doctrines that these men taught, they must still admit that there is scarcely any Protestant doctrine that is not to be encountered in a more or less developed form before the Reformation itself.

If Luther had forerunners, he also, secondly and quite obviously, had followers; to deny objectivity to a historical phenomenon such as Protestantism would be absurd. On the other hand, recognizing that Protestantism is really there profoundly alters the character of Catholicism. Catholicism can no longer claim to be absolute religious objectivity and truth, and should it continue to do so, it is deceptive. Protestantism, of course, also claims "to have in itself the principle of absolute truth,"[8] but with the vast difference that the visible church is not asserted to be the bearer and mediator of absolute truth except in a very secondary sense. For Protestantism, rather, it is the invisible church that is "the realm of absolute truth."[9] Hence for Protestantism the presence of many visible Protestant churches and also of Catholicism is no scandal at all. On the other hand, Catholicism can no more recognize another visible church in addition to itself than it can recognize another and independent absolute truth; herein lies the reason why Catholicism attempts to annihilate other visible churches. Despite all the efforts of Catholicism, however, Protestantism is firmly rooted in history, so firmly rooted that "Catholicism" is merely a nostalgic name for the Roman, or papist, communion. The Roman Church is no more wholly objective than the Protestant churches are wholly subjective; or again, what is obective in each is as old as Christianity itself. What is subjective in each has resulted in large part from their mutual opposition.

In the light of these reflections the distinctions that Möhler makes about the use of the writings of private theologians is quite senseless; if Catholicism, in the sense of Catholic dogma, is not absolute truth, there is no point in distinguishing it from the writings of individuals. Nor, in practice, does Möhler always do so, for he freely cites the *Catechismus Romanus* and wavers in his estimation of the dogmatic worth of certain papal pronouncements. On the other hand, how does the fact that a given statement happens to have been made by Luther affect its theological validity? Cannot the general and the objective come to consciousness in an individual, and moreover, does not the fact that a certain individual wins a large following provide an implicit evaluation of what he says? And must not a distinction be made, for any theologian, Catholic or Protestant, between what Luther passed on to others and what remained his own?

> In any case, no matter how much can be found in the personal writings of Luther that bears the character of Luther's personality, no matter how fortuitous, how arbitrary, or how subjective all this may be, it cannot be imputed to

[8]G^2, p. 37.
[9]*Ibid.*

Protestantism; for a system of which the first and highest principle in matters of faith is that no human authority ought to prevail can hardly hold Luther's authority to be unconditional. Protestantism presents Luther's highest and weightiest principles as true, not because Luther formulated and expressed them, but because, in themselves, they are true, and stand over every individual consciousness.[10]

Luther's views, as such, are scarcely the Protestant rule of faith! Even if one finds Luther's writings helpful in understanding the confessional literature of Protestantism—just as, for example, Möhler frequently finds Bellarmine helpful in expounding Catholicism—one must not neglect the Protestant confessions, as Möhler often does. No matter how useful Luther's or anyone else's personal writings may be in tracing the genesis of Protestantism, however, nothing must be attributed to the Protestant *churches* that is not found in their confessions. It is "unsymbolical," remakrs Baur, "to construct the symbolic doctrinal idea outside the symbols."[11]

It must not be thought, however, that the Protestant confessions are the norm of Protestant doctrine any more than the private writings of the Reformers. There is, for example, no guarantee that important Protestant doctrines contained in the private writings always made their way into the confessions as amply as might be desired. Conversely, all the doctrines found in the confessions "must always be tested, as to whether or not they correspond to the highest principle of Protestantism."[12] It is easy to see, Baur continues, that this highest principle of Protestantism cannot be simply that Protestant doctrine is what scripture authorizes it to be. This last is a purely formal criterion; what is needed is a material criterion, a rule for telling what doctrines, concretely, are found in scripture and are truly Protestant. Baur's elucidation of this basic Protestant principle now follows, in his text, in some ten closely reasoned pages; because of the crucial importance of this discussion for Baur's understanding of symbolics as well as of Protestantism itself—as well as for the reader's understanding of Baur—extensive quotations will be made.

Baur's point of departure for determining the "Protestant Principle" is borrowed from Schleiermacher. The only criterion that can stand in judgment over the personal writings of the Reformers, the confessions, and even scripture itself is some kind of inner criterion, some determination of consciousness.

What Schleiermacher says in this respect about Christianity—that something is not Christian because it stands in the writings of the New Testament, but rather stands therein because it is Christian—must in like manner hold for Protestantism. Thus, just as there is a Christian consciousness, there must also

[10]G^2, pp. 44f.

[11]G^2, p. 47.

[12]G^2, p. 48.

[13]*Ibid.*

be a primordial Protestant consciousness, the affirmations of which are the guiding norm for all the externally given.[13]

The question now arises as to how "we attain this consciousness, or the principle that determines it." One would be tempted to say, like Schleiermacher, by being, or becoming, Protestant. Baur does not quite follow Schleiermacher here, however, and in a rather more intellectualist manner replies, "Without doubt, by, from the most characteristic doctrines of Protestantism, abstracting the general standpoint of Protestantism."[14] And what is this general standpoint? "The central point of Protestantism is formed by the two basic Christian doctrines of sin and grace;... nothing is more opposed to basic Protestantism than all that which can be understood under the general name of Pelagianism."[15]

It can be said, then, that the basis of Protestantism and of Protestant opposition to Pelagianism is the doctrine that no human works and merits are of salvific value before the absolute holiness and justice of God. Still, the inquiry after the Protestant principle can be carried a step further. Why is nothing human of salvific value before God? "The answer," replies Baur, "is simply this, that, in general, the human is, before God, in itself nothing." What Baur apparently means is that to consider man as being capable of existing and acting independently of God is to enter upon a line of thought that simply has no referent in extra-conceptual reality; when Baur says "nothing" he means, not metaphorically, but literally, ontologically *nothing*. A creature that were to be in any sense independent of God would be a contradiction in terms and an impossibility in reality. In terms of Pelagianism, the sort of freedom propounded by the Pelagians is an illusion, "for he who is free is he who determines himself through himself, who has in himself the principle of his acting."[16]

It is true, of course, that the foregoing definition of freedom can be interpreted in an acceptable sense, namely that God moves man to move himself. In this case man might be said to have a sort of partial spontaneity, but never that sort of spontaneity by which man might, quite independently of God, do whatever he chose. The Pelagians have this second, actually dualistic, freedom in mind. Baur explains—

> No matter how unlike and separate are the principles that constitute this dualism, so long as the subordinate principle remains free in the sense of being self-subsistent and independent, the thesis that maintains that outside God there can be nothing in itself good no longer holds, for with freedom comes also the possibility of a good outside God. If however, there is outside God a power for good, which power subsists for itself, then the thesis that maintains that all good can only be caused by God no longer holds.[17]

[14]*Ibid.*
[15]G^2, pp. 48f.
[16]G^2, p. 49.
[17]G^2, pp. 49f.

It is thus essential to the Protestant consciousness that nothing be asserted to exercise independent causality; in the real order absolutely nothing limits the divine causality.

As might be supposed, the point of defining Protestantism against Pelagianism is that Catholic Christian anthropology is a continuation of Pelagianism. Catholicism dualistically envisions man as free in the sense of being partially independent from God. In the Catholic conception of man and his freedom, God and man stand over against each other as two unequal, to be sure, but still independent sources of initiative. In the production of good they are meant to work together, and throughout this common work man is able clearly to distinguish his causality from that of God, if not in consciousness, at least in *a posteriori* metaphysical or theological reasoning. Because Catholicism creates for man his own little sphere of activity, Catholicism must then consider grace as something external to man, a travesty of what it really is. Because man is thought to have his own little sphere, the divine causation that touches the inmost center of his being appears to be something but extrinsically related to it.

According to Protestantism and in reality, Baur continues, grace absolutely must be conceived as an inner, immanent divine influence. In a passage of signal value for understanding his conception of Protestantism Baur sets forth the ideal God-man relationship:

> The stronger it [Protestantism] works out its opposition to Pelagianism, the more necessary does it become to think of divine grace as an essential and necessary principle of human being and acting, apart from which the latter has no objective worth. It is primarily a question of the good in itself, without which man cannot have any objective worth before God or truly substantial principle of life in himself. But does it not necessarily result that the human spirit is altogether for itself the finite, created, and individual spirit, and has its true spiritual life only in its identity with God as the absolute spirit—which absolute spirit is what it is only because it is, in all finite created spirits (which by the homogeneity of all spiritual life in itself must be one with the absolute spirit), the immanent cause of their spiritual being and acting? The human spirit, however, càn be one with the divine spirit only in so far as what it has of the finite, the created, and the individual-in-itself is considered the transcended-and-cancelled. The individual has its natural unity in the universal. The individual spirit, therefore, knows itself to be one with the universal spirit of humanity, which, as the natural mediator between God and man, is of both divine and human nature, that is, of divine-human nature.[18]

Baur is perfectly aware that many term this sort of religious thought pantheism, but he is equally aware that those who are not disturbed by mere labels will recognize that an anti-Pelagian position on the causality of grace leads to no other conclusion but this.

As a matter of fact the appellation "pantheism" is with better logic applied to Catholicism. If one prescinds from the idea of immanent causality—which,

[18]G^2, pp. 51f.

after all, is a perfectly legitimate sense of "pantheism"—and conjures up what might be a "pantheist" view of the universe, what is the result? Is it not a picture of the universe as a giant, artfully contrived, and therefore "divine" aggregate, a kind of quasi-organism made of interrelated parts, with a special place and function for each part? And yet what is this but the hierarchical structure of Catholicism? Even the God of Catholicism is simply the highest point and guarantor of the world order that reaches down from him to pope to layman. Nonetheless, through this pantheistic preoccupation with an *external* hierarchy Catholicism succeeds in suppressing all thought of *internal* dependence on God; one is, in practice, dependent on the church. Church, and world, generally, thus come to take the place of the *true* God, indeed, by reason of man's alleged freedom, to stand over against him. It is impossible actually, to make sense of Catholicism; in combination, the dubiously coherent Catholic ideas of freedom and hierarchy seem to demand a world-view that is at once pantheistic and dualistic.

In Catholicism, in short, man is immersed in the immediate, in the first, unanalyzed dreams and impressions recorded in consciousness. In his illusory ability to stand over against God he conceives himself to have "in his nature a side of his essence in respect to which he does not need to become, but already is, what, according to the idea of man, he ought to be."[19] In Protestantism, on the other hand,

> the human, as opposed to God, the absolute, is so very much utter nothingness that it simply cannot persist in what it immediately is, but, through an endless process of mediation becomes what, according to its idea, it ought to be. The human has its truth only in the fact that it is a moment of the manifestation of the divine.[20]

Because in Protestantism, therefore, all depends on God and is a manifestation of God, *Protestantism is progressive*; just as because in Catholicism man is thought to be, of himself, in part at least, what his nature calls him to be, Catholicism is conservative, if not stagnant.

> Whereas in this respect Catholicism holds fast to the positivity of immediacy, Protestantism, through the inner negativity of the idea, which it has in itself as a moving principle, is driven from one moment of mediation to another. As in the former, therefore, there is being persisting in remaining at rest, in the latter there is becoming grasped in its very movement.[21]

Of such a nature, Baur concludes, is Protestantism when seen, correctly, in the light of the Protestant principle of the omni-causality of divine grace. Only from

[19] G^2, p. 55.
[20] G^2, pp. 55f.
[21] G^2, p. 56.

such a standpoint as that sketched here can the real meaning of the Protestant confessions be grasped. Had Möhler read both the confessions and the personal writings of the Reformers from this point of view, instead of emphasizing the immediate, subjective, fortuitous, and even conflicting elements in these texts, he would indeed have deserved to be considered a scientific symbolist. Unfortunately, he is only another polemicist, who must now, point by point, further be exposed for what he is.

Original Justice and Original Sin

Chapter I of the *Gegensatz* takes up the Doctrine of Sin and the Original Nature of Man. The chapter is divided into three sections, which deal in turn with Möhler's misuse of Protestant texts, with the relative value, in general, of Catholic and Protestant Christian anthropology, and with, in particular, the opposing positions on the, nature of freedom. Baur agrees with Möhler that it would have suited Möhler's case better to have begun with the doctrine of the church, and that it is more favorable to Protestants to begin with the doctrines of original justice and original sin. Nonetheless, Baur does not wish to begin to reply to Möhler on the subject of original justice because "in itself it lies outside the sphere of the religious consciousness."[22] Since original justice can, in any case, only be understood by inference from original sin, Baur may as well begin with original sin.

The reason why Möhler finds the Protestant conception of original sin and its consequences "ohne Sinn und Verstand" is simply that he has misunderstood them.[23] The question is, as Möhler has correctly seen, "whether man in the state of original sin is still man, that is, a morally reasonable being, and not rather a purely animal, or indeed, diabolical being."[24] Now Möhler has misunderstood the Protestant position to the extent of believing that the latter is the case.

What proofs does Möhler advance for his views? It will be recalled that Möhler cited the Apology for the Augsburg Confession to the effect that in original sin man lost the possibility and gift of trusting in God. From this and other texts Möhler concluded that, for Protestantism, man's rational powers have been seriously damaged, if not altogether effaced. Baur now replies that the lines quoted by Möhler have been quoted out of context. In the text cited from the Apology Melanchthon was writing against those who had asserted that in the state of original sin man can yet so act as to be completely pleasing to God. The following lines from the same passage make this point clear: Melanchthon disagrees with those theologians who "attribute to human nature unimpaired power

[22]G^2, p. 62.
[23]G^2, pp. 60-81.
[24]G^1, p. 20; G^2, p. 66.

to love God above all things and to obey his commandments." These theologians do not see that they are contradicting themselves.

> To be able to love God above all things by one's own power and to obey his commandments, what else is this but to have original righteousness? If human nature has such powers that by itself it can love God above all things, as the scholastics confidently assert, then what can original sin be?[25]

Thus, Baur argues, to say that man cannot be completely pleasing to God hardly means that man has lost a substantial part of his nature. It is simply a verbal fiction to say that, by reason of the unity of the concept *justice,* if only *civil* justice is now possible for man therefore *no* justice is possible for him. It is the same as concluding that the man who cannot equal the poetic achievements of Homer has no poetic sense at all.

Baur makes the same judgment about Möhler's quotation from the Formula of Concord in which man is said to lack any *modus agendi* with respect to *res spirituales.* How can Möhler conclude that this text means that man has quite lost his reason? Another text from the same document states quite the opposite: "It is . . . true that prior to his conversion man is still a rational creature with an intellect and will."[26] What Möhler fails to do is to distinguish between the weakened state of a faculty and its complete absence. If because of its weakened state reason is confined to the finite world as its circle of activity, there is no cause for saying that it has completely ceased to function. In fact, to make clear their position regarding the corruption of man's higher powers, the authors of the Formula of Concord explicitly presupposed their continued existence: "Although man's reason or natural intellect still has a dim spark of the knowledge that there is a God, as well as of the teaching of the law (Rom. 1:19-21, 28, 32), nevertheless it is . . . ignorant, blind, and perverse . . . ."[27] In the light of this text it is, further, pointless of Möhler to adduce cases of virtue among the heathen; while not completely likening them to Christians reborn through grace, the Lutheran confessional documents have not the least mind to make brute beasts of them. To sum up, Baur notes that the underlying error of Möhler's presentation is one of mistaking a difference of degree for one of kind, of confusing the highest level of man's spiritual capabilities with man's spiritual capabilities generally. If Möhler is going to examine with such extreme rigor the language of the confessions, it is only fair that his own language be given the same attention.

When Möhler attempts to show that, in the Protestant view, original sin introduced something positively evil into man's nature, his arguments are similarly unconvincing. Whatever Luther, and above all, Matthias Flacius, had to say on

[25]G^2, p. 67 (*BK,* p. 149; Eng., pp. 101f.).

[26]G^2, p. 70 (*BK,* p. 895; Eng., p. 532).

[27]G^2, p. 74 (*BK,* p. 874; Eng., p. 521).

this subject must ever remain private opinion. The Formula of Concord expressly rejects the view that "since the Fall human nature is initially created perfect and pure, and that afterward Satan infuses and blends original sin (as something essential) into man's nature, as when poison is blended with water."[28] When Luther speaks of sin as being the *essence* of man, in any case, it must first be established that he intended to use this term in its strictest philosophical sense; Baur is of the opinion that this was not at all his intention. Rather, in the lines from the commentary on Genesis that Möhler quotes, Luther is arguing against the view that just as original justice can be taken from man *without altering his nature,* so original sin can come upon him and yet leave him unchanged. Luther's point, says Baur, is that original sin, whatever it is, seriously affects man; only in this sense, taking *nature,* or *essence,* in a wider, actually, empirical meaning, is original sin "something belonging to the very nature of man."[29]

Once the foregoing rather gratuitous misconceptions have been removed, the heart of the questions of original justice and original sin can be reached.[30] But first a clear definition of original sin must be set forth. Baur suggests the following:

> Original sin designates that state of man in which, in so far as it is considered for itself, the higher-spiritual consciousness and life which is imparted to man only through the divine principle of Christianity has not yet been awakened. All that belongs to the side of man that is merely sensuous, purely natural, and not yet aroused by the spirit is just for this reason ruled and penetrated by original sin. What is essential to the concept of original sin consists in this: a state in itself natural is at the same time considered to be a sinful state, that is, a state, not original, but first originating through man's own fault, as an alteration of man's nature for which man himself is responsible. With the concept of nature that of sin must be joined . . . .[31]

Original sin is thus how the present state of man's nature, considered apart from grace, is reflected in the Christian consciousness. Baur will now examine in turn the Catholic and Protestant doctrinal positions to evaluate how they give propositional form to this consciousness.

The positions of both Catholics and Protestants presuppose a state of original justice anterior to that of original sin; they differ, however, over whether what constituted man in that state belonged to his nature or not. The latter position has been the common one among Catholics, but, as Möhler notes, it has never been defined as dogma. Möhler suggests that the fathers of Trent wanted to leave room for further speculation on the part of theologians, but Baur thinks

[28]G^2, p. 79 (*BK,* p. 852; Eng., p. 512).
[29]G^1, p. 29; G^2, p. 80.
[30]G^2, pp. 82-118.
[31]G^1, p. 30; G^2, pp. 80f.

that the fundamental contrariness of the traditional Catholic position prevented any progression along the same line. The view that man's nature is the same after the fall as before seems, first, to imply that in man God has created a creature whose nature is composed of inharmonious elements—an assertion for which no good reason can be given. Secondly, it is difficult to see how this position differs from that of the Pelagians, for if man's nature remains thus constant, there can hardly have been an original sin of any magnitude; if there is no original sin, however, there is no need of redemption in Christ and—if one is Catholic—in the church. Thirdly, if man's nature so remains the same, then the supernatural, through which man achieves what must be the perfection of his being, must be conceived as extrinsic to man. Fourthly, it seems as if the fall of man must be ascribed not to man's will, but rather to God's withdrawal of the supernatural helps that man had hitherto enjoyed. In the fifth place, to say that man's nature is the same after the fall as before suggests, overall, a rather low estimate of man's nature. In the sixth place, to follow out the same thought, a kind of dualism is introduced into one's understanding of the God-man relationship, since in some way man's lower powers are able to rebel against reason and yet not be found to be acting in a manner at variance with man's nature. In the seventh place, by this view man is completely put out of relationship with his end; there is left no point of contact by which he might be in a position to receive help for his infinite task. In the eighth place, this view necessitates calling grace an accident, and therefore involves calling the whole economy of salvation an accident. Finally, this view implies that supernatural help is dependent upon man's consent to it. If this is the result of the freedom of research provided by the fathers of Trent, Baur adds, "we have no reason to envy Catholic minds their freedom."[32]

Turning now to the Protestant answer to the question of whether all of what man had in the state of original justice belonged to his nature, Baur objects to how Möhler relates Luther and the scholastics. It is basically irrelevant whether Luther took his doctrine about the essentiality of original justice from the scholastics, or whether, for the sake of preaching, he chose the least complicated scholastic opinion. All that matters is whether Luther's doctrine corresponds to the gospel, and there are good grounds for holding that it does. Avoiding the difficulties of the Catholic position, it immediately sets forth a much more noble picture of man; that from which man has come and to which he is destined to return is his by nature, not something extrinsically added to his nature. Man, by nature, had, has, and will have the divine in him:

> If ... Protestantism is wont to proceed very critically in distinguishing and keeping separate the divine and the human where both have an external tendency to flow into each other and become mixed, nevertheless, in accordance with its innermost nature, Protestantism seeks, *inwardly*, in the spirit of man himself, to apprehend the divine and the human in their unity, although

[32]G^1, p. 53; G^2, p. 110.

at the same time it does not seek to cancel the essential difference of the one and the other.[33]

A second reason for the superiority of Luther's understanding of original justice is that it is a truer, more accurate conceptualization of the God-man relationship; if it avoids externalism, it also avoids the periodization that such externalism causes. If one conceives of man as developing organically, through his own inner law, one must also hold that from the beginning there are enclosed in man those principles of which the mutual opposition manifests itself in the course of life, and of which the gradual victory of one brings man, stepwise, to the realization of his highest potentialities. "According to this view," Baur continues,

> all that man becomes through divine grace in Christ can only be a develop-
> ment, implied in his own nature, to the highest level of truly personal and
> spiritual life, without which human nature would lack the completion includ-
> ed in its concept. The Christian consciousness and life that man has in him can
> only be the principle of his higher spiritual life as an integral, substantial
> element of his essence, which, just as surely as God has become man in Christ,
> cannot be alien to his nature or come into it from the outside.[34]

Of course, this is all a modern paraphrase of classical Protestant doctrine, and yet, Baur notes, recent Protestant thinkers have done well by their tradition. In its essentials this doctrine is identical with that of Luther; in his commentary on Genesis, as noted above, Luther taught that original righteousness was natural to man, that is, that it belonged to Adam's nature to believe in God and to love him.[35] As Schleiermacher has said so well, Christ is both natural and super-natural, in a word, the completed creation of human nature. There must, after all, be a parallel between Christ and what he brings—and those to whom it is brought. The view that the constituents of original justice are extrinsic to human nature coheres only with a Nestorian Christology; only the Protestant and orthodox position allows for the homogeneity and unity of consciousness of both the redeemer and the redeemed.

Freedom

Baur reserves for special examination what he considers "the central point . . . around which . . . this whole controversy moves"—the question of free-dom.[36] Freedom, as Möhler correctly noted, was the issue closest to the hearts of the Counter-Reformers, since unless man is free human dignity is immeasur-

[33]G^1, p. 55; G^2, p. 114.
[34]G^1, p. 56; G^2, p. 115.
[35]G^2, pp. 115f.
[36]G^1, p. 60; G^2, p. 119.

ably lessened and the evil we experience and do must be attributed directly to God. The issue of freedom is no less important for Baur, however, since, if he wishes to base his understanding of the God-man relationship upon the data of the Christian consciousness, he must explain satisfactorily why we *do* feel that we have the power to shape our lives and that we are responsible for what we do. Here, if anywhere, the Catholic position appears to be preferable to Baur's Protestantism.

Baur begins his discussion of freedom by conceding that the Lutheran confessional documents do not handle the question at all well.[37] The Augsburg Confession states that "the cause of sin is the will of the wicked;... as soon as God withdraws his support, the will turns away from God to evil."[38] The Formula of Concord reaffirms the same position: "The reason for such contempt of the Word is not God's fore-knowledge but man's own perverse will, which rejects or perverts the means and instrument of the Holy Spirit which God offers to him . . . ."[39] In this connection the Augsburg Confession also states:

> All men have a free will . . . . However, this does not enable them, without God, to begin or (much less) to accomplish anything in those things which pertain to God, for it is only in acts of this life that they have freedom to choose good or evil.[40]

The difficulty that these texts raise, argues Baur, is that although man can choose between alternatives only in matters pertaining to this present life, man is nevertheless said to be able to refuse divine grace and so to sin through his own fault. But then, if some men are damned through their own fault, what can one conclude except that for those who are saved

> the cause thereof is primarily that they do not withstand the workings of the Spirit, but . . . allow the Spirit to be efficaciously active in them; and if this presupposes in man himself a certain inner movement and capability for the good, a receptivity, even if only passive, for the divine, so can this still not be thought of without a free activity of the will.[41]

Because the Lutheran confessional documents do not want to choose between Catholic synergism and the Calvinist assertion of exclusively divine causality, they involve themselves in contradiction. In as much as·an understanding of human freedom that allows man in any sense to determine God is clearly Pelagian and anti-Protestant, one must conclude, then, that "the Reformed Church, which in so many ways more authentically worked out the principle of

[37]G^2, pp. 118-26.

[38]G^2, p. 121 (*BK*, p. 75; Eng., pp. 40f.).

[39]G^2, p. 122 (*BK*, p. 1076; Eng., p. 623).

[40]*Ibid.* (*BK*, p. 73; Eng., pp. 39f.).

[41]G^1, p. 64; G^2, p. 123.

the Reformation," did so here, too.[42]

That the clearly anti-Pelagian orientation of Reformed doctrine suggests the best line of response to the question of freedom is reinforced by the fact that the remaining alternatives to Reformed clarity and Lutheran muddledness are of no value whatever. Baur examines in turn the free-will position and also Augustine's position.

Free will in the sense of *liberum arbitrium* may be defined as "the power to decide in like manner for one thing as for another, for good as for evil."[43] There are two difficulties with this view. The first is that of the relativizing of the absolute good. If, out of man's inherent goodness he can choose the absolute good, there would seem to be two sources of good, not, as there must be, only one. Only the absolute good, strictly speaking, can be called good, "and everything else, for the reason that it does not have such a worth, is not truly to be named good." From the point of view of the indifference that the *liberum arbitrium* is alleged to possess, however,

> the absolute measure of the good is placed, not in the object, but only in the subject which determines itself either for good or for evil; and now all that is to be named good for which the self-determining subject decides, since its decision is for what appears good and reasonable to it according to its subjective outlook.[44]

Thus, in effect, the norm of goodness is no longer the absolute good but the choosing subject—and in the end one cannot be sure where the good lies.

The second difficulty with the concept of the *liberum arbitrium* is that it does not really correspond so closely with our moral self-consciousness as might be thought. Freedom in this sense does not admit of degrees: either one is free or one is not. Nonetheless, experience tells us that the human personality does in fact grow by degrees; no one swings wildly from goodness to badness and back. Nor is anyone's power of choice ever, like a scale, in a state of complete indifference, or balance. We choose what we in fact find good or reasonable, and the aggregate of our choices coalesces into what we term our character. What appear at first to be discrete free choices are conditioned by character and outlook.

Augustine's attempt at resolving the question of the meaning of freedom is similarly wanting.[45] Augustine stated that though man had complete freedom before the fall, after the fall he does not. The problem with Augustine's view is that he cannot explain how this free choice on Adam's part could result in such extraordinary consequences both for Adam himself and for his offspring. The only possible link between the one deed of Adam and all its results is a miracu-

---

[42]G^1, p. 67; G^2, p. 126.

[43]G^1, pp. 67f.; G^2, p. 126. Regarding *liberum arbitrium*, see G^2, pp. 126-30.

[44]G^1, p. 69; G^2, p. 128.

[45]G^2, pp. 130-37.

lous intervention of divine omnipotence. The only trouble is that then "there can scarcely be another theory in which God appears to be more immediately the author of moral evil than the Augustinian."[46]

It is therefore erroneous to say that Luther, and Calvin, who gave Luther's basic insight a more coherent expression, were simply returning to the teaching of Augustine. They do, of course, agree with Augustine that the relation of man to God is one of absolute dependence, but they base their dependence on a different sort of reasoning. This sort of reasoning, the core of the Reformers' teaching, forms the basis of Baur's response to Möhler in the *Gegensatz*.

Baur's argument here proceeds in three steps, each of which will be, by reason of its interest and import, presented with ample quotations from Baur's own text.[47] Baur's first step is the presentation of what he takes to be the kernel of the Reformers' outlook. How did the Reformers arrive at the feeling of absolute dependence on God?

> If this unconditional dependence cannot be derived from a free act of man, so must it, with the act itself, be traced back to the absolute being of the Deity; and that act can remain worthy of consideration only in so far as in it the universal dependence of man's being in its relation to God comes to the fore. If, however, the fall of man is already predestined by God, it is completely unessential to think of it as an act that happened at a definite time; it is as eternal as the very nature of man. What, according to Augustine is a self-subsistent act posited through its own power is, according to Luther and Calvin, only an external appearance in which an in itself already posited relationship of man to God only becomes fixed for consciousness. Man is what he is only through God's eternal idea of his essence, out of which, as the eternal unity, comes forth all that only for the temporal consciousness of man temporally falls asunder. Man's creation, his fall, and his redemption are only the mutually conditioning moments in which the essence of man, as it is in itself determined by God, comes forth into the external appearance of its temporal being.[48]

It is only this view, not that of Augustine, Baur continues, that forms the real opposite of the Pelagian conception of the *liberum arbitrium*. As a result, the Reformers chose this view; after having given the *basis* of the Protestant view of freedom, Baur will now, in the second point of his argument, discuss just how the Reformers *expressed* it. Even if the Reformers' basic principle was that of divine omni-causality, or conversely, man's absolute dependence on God, it must nevertheless be recognized that since "for the Reformers the moral and religious

---

[46]G^1, p. 77; G^2, p. 135.

[47]G^2, pp. 138-73. Most of Baur's textual emendations occur in this section. It is important to note, however, that there are a sufficient number of Hegelian-sounding passages already present in G^1 to suggest that Baur was strongly influenced by Hegel at the time of its composition.

[48]G^1, p. 79; G^2, p. 139.

interest prevailed over, and outweighed all others,"[49] the Reformers formulated the foregoing view in a manner different from that in which it has been present- ed here. Baur recognizes that what has been presented here must, in the light of historical fact, be regarded as an expansion of what the Reformers said. None- theless, the Reformers' more ethical language leads directly into Baur's more speculative language:

> The center-point from which the Reformers formed their whole system remains ever the deepest consciousness of the sinfulness of human nature, or the complete incapacity of man for producing out of himself not only some- thing relatively and subjectively good but also the good in itself, which alone merits the name of good. . . . Nothing more stands in the way of giving the fullest expansion to the divine omnipotence and to the divine will, which last is bound to no fore-knowledge and absolutely efficacious. It is clear that the doctrine of Luther and Calvin can be correctly perceived only from this point of view.[50]

Baur now quotes a number of passages from Luther's and Calvin's writings to back up his contention that what he presents is truly their teaching. The most important of them is from Luther's *De Servo Arbitrio,* wherein Luther argues that God's foreknowledge is the conditioning, not the conditioned, element in future events; God is in no sense bound by a foreknowledge of what his creatures will do, but rather knows already what he will cause them to do.[51] Baur remarks of the famous *horribile decretum* passage in Calvin's *Institutes* that it would better have served its purpose of consoling and drawn fewer attacks had Calvin's manner of expression been less immediately practical and more speculative.[52]

Luther and Calvin clearly deny that free will in the sense of *liberum arbitrium* is possible. They must therefore affirm, it would seem, that, since evil is clearly present, God is the cause of evil: "If man is simply dependent on God, it certainly seems equally correct to trace all good to divine activity and to find the effective cause of all evil only in God."[53] The Reformers, however, do not affirm God to be the cause of evil; they rather affirm just the opposite, namely that, in Calvin's words, "Man falls as God's providence ordains, but he falls by his own fault."[54] Have the Reformers contradicted themselves, and must one in the end confess that they are, on the whole, no more coherent than the *Book of Concord*?

Of course not. Everything, rather, depends on one's idea of evil. In the

---

[49] G^1, pp. 80f.; G^2, pp. 140f.

[50] G^1, p. 82; G^2, pp. 142f.

[51] G^2, pp. 140f.

[52] G^2, p. 142.

[53] G^1, p. 84; G^2, p. 145.

[54] G^2, p. 145. (Battles' translation, II, 957.)

following summary passage Baur sets forth the fundamental insight of his whole discussion of freedom, evil, original justice and original sin:

> If the fall can be thought of only as a deterioration of a nature originally created pure and good by God, so is the fall, or the evil that enters the nature through the fall, related to the nature itself as the negative to the positive. We must distinguish here a negative and a positive side of human nature. All that belongs to the positive side is the nature created by God. What, on the other hand, is the negative in the positive cannot be traced back to the same divine activity as the positive, since it must be treated only as the denial and the limit of the creative activity of God with respect to man. What, therefore, can Calvin's proposition, 'Man falls as God's providence ordains, but he falls by his own fault,' mean except only this: In so far as he is created by God man is truly pure and good, but there is also a finite side of his being that is turned away from God and therefore perverted and evil? As on the one side he bears the image of God itself, so has he on the other a fallen nature. Now for the reason that, if he is to be man, he cannot be thought of otherwise than with this negativity and finitude of his being—which fully inserts him into the opposition of the infinite and the finite, the perfect and the imperfect, the positive and the negative, the good and the evil—the fall is his own fault. It is thus the primordial sin, and man is responsible for it, in as much as this negativity and finitude, which is the source of all the evil in him, so belongs to the concept of his being that it cannot be separated from it. For this reason, at least according to the idea, the fall must be posited as equally eternal with the nature of man.[55]

To suggest without further qualification, therefore, that the fall need not have occurred is indiscriminately to mix imaginative and truly speculative elements. The heart of the presentation of the fall as something historical, free, and fortuitous lies rather in the thought that the fall, precisely as such, is the passage from the ideal to the real-historical.

> In the identity of man with God is also at once posited his differentiation from God, with all the moments through which the divine idea of man as a being developing in time realizes itself, in order to transcend and cancel the being-for-himself of man into his being-in-himself. Both the one and the other are ordained by God. Still, it is the sole fault of man that the idea of human nature can be realized only through the mediation of the fall and sin.[56]

It must be emphasized, however, that throughout this whole chain of reasoning evil, or negativity, means, quite literally, *nothing,* "that to which," if one may so speak, the divine causality does not reach:

[55] G^1, pp. 85f.; G^2, pp. 146f. The text is identical in the two editions.

[56] G^1, p. 88; G^2, pp. 148f. The first sentence quoted here is lacking in G^1; what follows is identical in both editions (the antecedent of "both" being man's power for good and power for evil, at least in G^1). Baur's point, I believe, is this: man's "fault" lies not in his having somehow degenerated, but precisely in his—structurally and necessarily—coming to consciousness, to self-realization, as, so to say, the less-than Absolute.

... Evil has its ground only in this, that the divine activity although in itself it extends at the same time to infinity, confines and limits itself at a definite point, in order with this limit to make room for finitude. If on one hand man is supported by the divine omnipotence, on the other he is only a finite and limited being.[57]

Such, says Baur, is what underlies Calvin's statements that when divine light is taken away nothing remains but darkness and blindness, that when his spirit is taken away our hearts turn to stone.[58] Such is what grounds Luther's assertion that though God uses evil men he himself does not do evil.[59] Provided one understands that evil is really finitude, the price for the realization of the divine idea of man, one understands as well the Reformers' insistence that, though God is exclusively the cause of man, he is not the cause of evil. For *what exists* is man, not evil.

And yet ... man *will* speak of evil. Men experience evil. The third and final point of Baur's argument here involves the reconciliation of the foregoing speculation with the data of the Christian consciousness. The answer to the apparent dilemma occasioned by the differing reports from consciousness and speculation is really quite simple. Says Baur: "God wills evil, not as evil, but only for the sake of the good; ... what from the finite standpoint appears as evil is in itself, from the higher, absolute standpoint, not evil, but good."[60] That we experience evil as evil is due only to the "subjectivity of the human consciousness."[61] This short-sightedness becomes especially apparent when the subject of reprobation comes up. What, after all, does it mean to be damned? If anything is evil, surely damnation is; and if any persons are evil, surely the damned must be. Baur replies that one must simply concede that Calvin went too far here; Schleiermacher shows much more speculative sensitivity. Is it not more reasonable to say, with Schleiermacher, that humanity is to be treated as a collectivity within which there are an infinity of degrees of grace?[62] From God's point of view evil is only non-being, and hence those who are said to suffer here or in eternity are really only those whose experience of finitude has become acute—and such a situation is meant gradually to be remedied by the grace of Christ. Did not Calvin suggest as much with his emphasis on the gradually disappearing cleavage between flesh, or the natural, and spirit, or the properly Christian?

What are we to conclude from this whole discussion? It is not all that easy,

---

[57] G^1, p. 90; G^2, p. 151. Text identical.

[58] G^2, p. 150.

[59] G^2, p. 152.

[60] G^2, pp. 160f.; lacking in G^1, though on pp. 98f. similar ideas are expressed.

[61] G^1, p. 95; G^2, p. 154.

[62] G^2, pp. 166f.

Baur admits: "If the idea of freedom in the full sense of the term cancels out the Christian absolute, the idea of absolute predestination, on the other hand, seeks to suppress the idea of freedom, against which suppression the moral consciousness of man struggles."[63] Still, remarks Baur, if something must be sacrificed, it had better be feelings which, upon examination, might prove to be less well founded than one had supposed. Man's moral consciousness would do better to struggle against the prideful idea of freedom in things of the spirit. According to the fundamental determination of the Christian consciousness, that which can under no circumstances be denied, man is unconditionally dependent upon God.

In his discussions of justification (Chapter II of the *Gegensatz*) and the sacraments (Chapter III) it is evident that Baur is in essential agreement with Möhler's structuring of Christian theology, to wit, that divergences of opinion as to the fall have a decisive influence on one's conception of redemption from its effects.[64] Paradoxically, perhaps, just because fallen man is unconditionally dependent upon God, and does not, *toward God,* enjoy freedom in the usual sense of the term, fallen man is completely free *in the intra-human exercise of religion,* free, that is, from bondage to human authority. That Christ is sacramentally present to redeemed man by no means entails the synergistic, hierarchically prescribed Catholic sacrament: the Lord's Supper, that is, need not degenerate into the sacrifice of the Mass. Because, in the things of God, men are, not doers, but receivers, it follows that no man can be a sacerdotal-sacramental *authority* for other men. In his discussion of the church (Chapter IV) Baur stresses that Protestantism is founded on the

> principle of freedom of belief and conscience, or the principle that, with respect to what concerns his relationship to God and Christ, no individual needs an external mediation—since even such a mediation as might be given through the visible church would make him dependent upon a human authority. To this principle is immediately joined that of the exclusive authority of holy scripture.[65]

In other words, scripture (including such directives as it gives regarding sacramental rites) quite adequately states the *true* organic relationship between the divine and the human. Continuing divine creativity founds the one, organic wholeness of God and man, not the alleged divine "afterthought" of Catholic priestly rite. The dignity of man lies in his capability of accepting and worshiping the divine

---

[63]G^1, p. 108; G^2, p. 171. In G^1 the first clause of the sentence quoted reads, "If the idea of freedom in the full sense of the term places Christianity on too subordinate a level . . . ." If in G^1 Christianity is implicitly compared with superficial ethical systems, in G^2 it is quite simply, and confidently, affirmed to be the absolute that cannot be cancelled or transcended, or more precisely, the complex of conditions under which man can best come into conscious relationship with the absolute.

[64]G^1, p. 110; G^2, p. 215.

[65]G^1, p. 329; G^2, p. 472. Further discussion of Baur's understanding of justification, sacraments, and the church may be found in *MBC,* Chap. V, pp. 181-218.

in spirit and truth, not in his pretending that he can add something to the divine initiative. But, in terms of history, man attains self-comprehension slowly and painfully. That is, to comprehend Catholic synergism one need only locate it in the history of western man's religious progress.

Conclusion: General Comparison of Catholicism and Protestantism

"Der Gegensatz der beiden Systeme im Allgemeinen" is the subject of the fifth and final chapter of Baur's *Gegensatz*. In this chapter, after having reviewed each doctrine in detail, Baur now undertakes to situate the differences between Catholicism and Protestantism within the overall process of western man's religious development, and by so doing, to demonstrate the legitimacy of the Protestant understanding of man.

Möhler, in his own general comparison of the two systems, has compared Protestantism to Gnosticism.[66] Baur replies, first, that Möhler's understanding of the origin and nature of Gnosticism is not entirely convincing. No matter how Gnosticism came to be, however, there is a great gulf between it and Protestantism. Protestantism holds to a strictly moral concept of evil; evil is sin, and sin, if not always an actual deed, is always at least a state of affairs for which man is responsible. Gnosticism, on the contrary, at least in its most common form, held that the root of evil is matter, considered as a principle independent of God. The source of evil in man is man's body. "All, therefore, that constitutes the great difference between the physical (or from a higher point of view, the metaphysical) and the ethical concepts of evil serves to distinguish Protestantism from Gnosticism."[67]

On the other hand, it cannot be denied that there is a certain plausibility in Möhler's comparison. Both Gnosticism and Protestantism, whatever their differences over the ultimate principle of evil, have stressed man's deep consciousness of evil and sin. It can even be said that Protestantism stands in relation to Catholicism as does Gnosticism to heathenism and Judaism. Both of the former members of this comparison have urgently sought a purification of man; both have a deeper desire for redemption than their predecessors. This proportion also means, however, that if there is a certain similarity between Protestantism and Gnosticism, there is also a similarity between Catholicism and heathenism-Judaism.

The only way to understand Catholicism is to examine its history:[68]

[66]G^2, pp. 541-46.

[67]G^1, p. 372; G^2, p. 545. The material in parentheses was added in G^2. By the *metaphysical* concept of evil Baur presumably means evil conceived as a positive, self-subsistent force; for the ethically perspicacious, evil is metaphysically, or entitively, nothing.

[68]G^2, pp. 546-70.

> As the history of Christianity is itself nothing else but the succession of attempts, made from the beginning onward, to mediate for consciousness the objective truth contained in Christianity, so is Catholicism the first large-scale attempt of this kind. In Christianity a new principle of truth was historically manifested, but what was divinely revealed could not immediately be acknowledged and apprehended in its purity. The new needed the mediation of the old.[69]

What Baur has in mind is that in the religious development of western man it was necessary that many of the forms of thought characteristic of pre-Christian religion carry over into Christianity. That the essence of Christianity, when it came into historical manifestation, could appear only "in that state of constraint implied in the relation of Christianity to older forms of religion" can hardly be denied. The result of this constraint is that "those forms served to develop and to bring to consciousness in the most varied manner possible the objective content of Christianity."[70]

The totality of those forms borrowed from pre-Christian religions yet mediating the full expansion of the Christian consciousness is none other than Catholicism. The principal phases of Catholicism are Alexandrian Platonism, Augustinianism, and medieval scholasticism. In Platonism Christianity borrowed from Greek thought. Even though the doctrines elaborated under the aegis of Platonism are generally thought to be the very basis of Christianity, Baur remarks, a closer examination of the history of doctrine reveals the radically unchristian character of Platonism in many ways. The unduly speculative Christology of Nicea, for example, had to be corrected—through a properly Christian reaction—by that of Chalcedon; and many Christians still do not see the cleavage between the Platonist doctrine of the fall and the immediate data of the Christian consciousness.

In Augustinianism the anthropological side of Christianity was developed; the extremely important Christian doctrines of sin and grace came to consciousness much more fully. Nevertheless, the manner in which Augustine set forth these doctrines was actually a borrowing from the Old Testament. If in an incipient fashion Augustine directed man's attention inwards, he nonetheless directed it back outwards again by his doctrine of the fall and its effects. Moreover, the difficulty Augustine encountered in explaining why Adam, who was free before the fall, became unfree after it, as well as why Adam's condition was passed on to his offspring led Augustine into an appeal to ecclesiastical authority. When the individual Christian was thus made dependent upon the tradition of the whole church, and principally upon a caste of episcopal teachers, Augustine ended by proclaiming, paradoxical as this may seem, a kind of occult Pelagianism: reliance on the church is, in the end, reliance on man.

---

[69]G^1, p. 374; G^2, pp. 546f.
[70]G^1, p. 375; G^2, p. 547.

Scholasticism, first with its emphasis on the power of reason and then with its loss of confidence in reason and consequent appeal to ecclesiastical authority, but above all with its invention of the *opus operatum,* developed the latent Pelagianism of Augustine. Throughout one's examination of pre-Reformation Christianity, however, it must ever be borne in mind that at no time did Christianity consider itself only a further development of essentially pre-Christian forms of religion.

Provided the identity of Christianity is not lost sight of, though, it is illuminating to reflect on the borrowings that took place. Platonist creation doctrine and Christology are essentially Greek; Augustinian and medieval doctrines of sin, grace, the church, and the role of reason are essentially heathen and Judaic. By the end of the middle ages all these borrowings had coalesced to give "to the Christianity of that time, on the whole, the appearance of heathenism."[71] What confronted the Reformers was a form of Christianity that had as its formal principle the authority of the church and as its material principle Pelagianism. What Protestantism did, while remaining part of the fundamental continuum, was to release the Christian consciousness from its bondage to pre-Christian forms of religion. Catholicism, of course, went its own reactionary and heathen way.

The Catholic response to this approach is to argue that the Reformation— and Protestantism—was and remains unjustified.[72] Baur disagrees. To begin with, what was needed was not a gradual improvement of the old order but a wholly new form of religious life. The basic question is really, not whether there should have been a division of Christianity, but whether the division that did in fact take place is justifiable in terms of essential Christianity—whether the ultimate religious authority is the hierarchy, or scripture as read by the Christian consciousness. The Protestant answer is clear enough. If yet more proof is needed, there is the simple fact that the attempts at reform before *the Reformation* did not, by the Catholics' own admission, succeed in removing the abuses in the church. Moreover, if the marks of the church, in Catholic fashion, are to be conceived somewhat externalistically, how can the historian be dissuaded from giving at least equal attention to both the Reformers and the pre-Reformation advocates of reform? Is it not meaningless to say that a valid religious revolution is impossible in principle? On what basis can such a statement be made?

The kind of conservative formalism dear to so many Catholics states flatly that any future reunion of the confessions must necessarily come about through the return of the Protestants to Mother Church.[73] What this view ignores is, of course, that such a return is totally foreign to the spirit of Protestantism, to what would be the *terminus a quo.* The Protestant cannot be enmeshed in the toils of sixteenth-century controversy, locked into his or anyone else's polemical

---

[71] G^1, p. 389; G^2, p. 561.

[72] G^2, pp. 570-85.

[73] G^2, pp. 585-99.

stance. Protestantism is progressive, and looks to Catholicism for sharers in a common life and a common labor. In regard to both religious life and religious thought, however, the true medium of the Spirit's action must not be forgotten. It is not external authority. It is, as Schleiermacher has labored so well to point out, the Christian consciousness. If the two confessions are ever to come together it must be on the basis of a common self-consciousness.

Recent philosophy may be of help here; in fact it has already become "in the highest degree influential" upon theology, for it

> sets speculative thought in the most intimate combination with the activity, objectified in history, of the spirit, in that it treats history as the living progress of the concept, or presents the absolute spirit as first through the mediation of history breaking through and rising to its own consciousness.[74]

The process of expanding consciousness may well include, in the not too distant future, a moment in which Protestantism and Catholicism will discover a common point of contact; for Catholicism it will mean release from bondage to the past, for Protestantism, a livelier grasp of tradition. Already there is hope; books like Möhler's *Einheit* bear undeniable traces of Schleiermacher's influence, and the writings of a number of young Catholic theologians demonstrate their authors' interest in the thought of Hegel.[75]

---

[74]G^1, pp. 431f.; G^2, p. 597.

[75]G^1, p. 436; G^2, p. 599. In G^1, pp. 436-39, Baur expresses his conviction that the eventual reunion of the confessions will be based, not on revived polemics, but on symbolics in the true sense of the term; Catholics should realize that freedom of conscience for both Protestants and themselves should not be the occasion for the revival of old hatreds.

Baur apparently envisions the emergence in his time of a new era in philosophy through the work of Hegel, and a new era in theology, at least *founded* (the word used is *begründen*), through the work of Schleiermacher. (G^1, p. 431; G^2, p. 597.) In neither edition of the *Gegensatz* does Baur explicitly state that Hegel, as a philosophical theologian, has *improved upon* Schleiermacher's theology—although this is exactly what Baur says in *Die christliche Gnosis*. See below, pp.

CHAPTER IV

The Knight in the Frock Coat

Möhler saw four editions of his *Symbolik* through the press and died while preparing a fifth edition. Baur reissued his *Gegensatz* in a second, notably expanded, edition. But Möhler had declined to encumber the *Symbolik* with new arguments against Baur, and had instead written a whole new book in defense of his first work, his *Neue Untersuchungen der Lehrgegensätze zwischen den Katholiken und Protestanten,* of which Möhler supervised two editions. Baur, for his part, replied to Möhler's *Neue Untersuchungen* with a lengthy article in the *Tübinger Zeitschrift für Theologie,* "Erwiederung auf Herrn Dr. Möhler's neueste Polemik . . . in der Schrift: *Neue Untersuchungen*"–which reply Baur to some extent incorporated into the second edition of his *Gegensatz.* The best way to examine the "second round" of the Möhler-Baur controversy would seem to be this: to consider (1) the second edition of Möhler's *Neue Untersuchungen*; (2) Baur's "Erwiederung"; (3) a non-controversial but highly enlightening work that Baur composed at the time of his interchange with Möhler, his *Die christliche Gnosis*; and (4) the immediate factual outcome of the controversy.

Möhler's Neue Untersuchungen

As the foregoing summaries of the contents of the *Symbolik* and the *Gegensatz* make quite evident, symbolics as practised by both Möhler and Baur includes two quite different undertakings. The first of these is, of course, to set down what the Reformers and Counter-Reformers had to say to each other. Once this has been done the second task of symbolics may be taken up, namely, the systematic interpretation and re-evaluation of the various sixteenth-century positions, in effect, a kind of symbolical higher criticism. In the introduction to the *Symbolik* Möhler states that for the symbolical theologian just as for the historian it does not suffice merely to set down the facts; rather must the facts be presented in terms of the organic unity to which they belong, which unity is to be discovered by a lively combination of further research and intuitive insight. The unity formed by each system of religious thought is then to be compared with the truths of right reason and the gospel.

As the foregoing chapters also make quite evident, however, "scientific" symbolics encountered certain embarrassments. In the light of reason and the gospel Möhler found the Protestant system to be "without sense and reason." Not surprisingly, perhaps, Baur found Möhler to be a rather questionable practitioner of symbolics. What was Möhler to do?

When the first installment of Baur's *Gegensatz* had appeared in the *Tübinger Zeitschrift für Theologie,* Möhler saw clearly enough both the character of Baur's defense of Protestantism as well as the most logical way to reply to it. Writing to his friend Adam Gengler on August 23, 1833, Möhler observes that

> Baur, no matter how obstinate his attack, has not frightened me. . . . Baur has already given up Lutheranism as untenable and attached himself to Calvinism as being more consistent—except that he has done so after the manner of Schleiermacher. On that account I am going to have sounded a hundred-and-one-gun salvo.[1]

Still, after the second installment of the *Gegensatz* had come out, Möhler's ardor had lessened somewhat. Writing to Gengler on October 19, 1833, he bemoans the presence of a really rainy day: he has caught a bad cold from his uncle in Rottenburg (a cause for some alarm, with winter coming and his health being as frail as it was), and he has just received the rest of *Der Gegensatz.* The work itself pleases him no more than before:

> His work is that of a typical Lutheran, opposed to Catholics, not in a dogmatic, but in a social and moral sense. He often badly misrepresents my presentation and then upbraids me for having given an inaccurate presentation of Protestantism, for having political designs, and so forth. He becomes especially coarse where the weaknesses of Protestantism cannot be covered over. Some good observations aside, the work as a whole has taken such a shape that I see myself confirmed in my whole view of Lutheranism from having read it. My principal objections have throughout not been touched. I should have thought that more would be said about them.
>
> I will reply—indeed, as soon as my work and my inclination to polemics permit. Still, I am in some perplexity as to how I should go about it: With the bluntness that he deserves would, I think, be detrimental to *the matter in hand,* as well as incompatible with my situation *here. Deus providebit* . . . .[2]

Symbolics itself may be in trouble, but, if he is not careful, Möhler may find himself in trouble not only with his colleagues on the Tübingen faculty but also, and worse, perhaps, with the king's ministers in Stuttgart. Nevertheless, not so very long after this rainy day God began to provide very well indeed.

Never, it would seem, did Möhler doubt that he would have to reply to Baur; his own honor and that of Catholicism demanded it. By December, 1833, he had decided that the most telling as well as the most politically astute way of answering Baur would be to expose him as a kind of theological fraud, in other

---

[1]Stefan Lösch, *Prof. Dr. Adam Gengler (1799-1866), die Beziehungen des Bamberger Theologen zu. J. J. J. Döllinger und J. A. Möhler: ein Lebensbild mit Beigabe von 80 bisher unbekannten Briefen, darunter, 47 neuen Möhler-Briefen* . . . (Würzburg: Schöningh, 1963), pp. 107f.

[2]*Ibid.,* p. 112.

words, to attack Baur, not Protestantism, and perhaps even to defend Protestantism from Baur. On December 10, 1833, he writes to Gengler:

> Against Baur's critique I shall very soon have ready a counter-critique of perhaps a length equal to Baur's. I have done what I think is some valuable research on this subject, which, I think, will on the whole demonstrate that Baur is almost less acquainted with Protestantism than he is with Catholicism.[3]

Soon his research was completed, and from the end of February to the middle of May, 1834, he composed his *Neue Untersuchungen der Lehrgegensätze zwischen den Katholiken und Protestanten: eine Vertheidigung meiner Symbolik gegen die Kritik des Herrn Professors Dr. Baur in Tübingen*.[4] By the end of June, 1834, the work was in the hands of the public, in an edition of 1500 copies. With the work completed, on June 24, 1834, Möhler writes in a rather more reflective frame of mind to Countess Sophie von Stolberg:

> I deeply regret that my work is not written up in a peaceful tone; I have become acquainted with a dark side of myself. . . .
>
> My adversary, Prof. Dr. Baur, had the idea, namely, to assert that the Reformers taught approximately the same as the most celebrated recent Protestant theologians. In order to make his point he blames me for having written the *Symbolik* out of impure motives and misrepresented the dogmas of the Reformers. This reproach greatly upset me, as is visible in the whole of my book. The fact remains, nevertheless, that my adversary, a well-known writer, found it necessary entirely to deny the doctrine of his confession in order to be able to defend it. As a result, his book was by no means a defense of his confession, but a public avowal that he considers it impossible to justify.[5]

What above have been called the two tasks of symbolics are clearly mirrored—and as clearly distinguished—in these excerpts from Möhler's correspondence. Möhler notes, first, that Baur accuses him of having distorted what the Reformers actually said, adding that in order to make such an accusation Baur himself must not be very well acquainted with their teaching. Secondly, Möhler continues, Baur tries to fit the teaching of the Reformers into a system of thought and experience where it simply does not belong; the teaching of

---

[3]Lösch, *Gengler*, p. 114.

[4]Lösch, *Gengler*, p. 108, n. 7. Cf. *Johann Adam Möhler*, Band I: *Gesammelte Aktenstücke und Briefe*, ed. Stephan (*sic*) Lösch (Munich: Kösel & Pustet, 1928), 188, 295. Vol. II, presumably a biography by Lösch, based on the sources collected in Vol. I, was, if written, never published; it was, however, advertised as forthcoming by the publishers.

[5]Möhler, *Aktenstücke und Briefe*, pp. 295f. In the preface to the fourth (1835) edition of the *Symbolik* Möhler remarks that the introduction of controversial material into that work would alter the form in which it has come before the public—changing its peaceful tone, he says, into a warlike one (*S*, p. 15).

Luther cannot be joined organically with that of Schleiermacher. Baur, as Möhler not unmaliciously put it, found it necessary to deny what might be called "classical Protestantism" in order to defend it.

These two lines of argumentation find ample expression in the *Neue Untersuchungen*. Möhler's reply to the *Gegensatz* follows Baur's work step by step. In four chapters devoted respectively to original justice and original sin, to justification, faith, and good works, to the sacraments, and to the church Möhler undertakes to refute in detail Baur's charge that he has misrepresented classical Protestantism. In a concluding chapter he counters Baur's observations on the general nature of Catholicism and on its place in history.

Throughout its more than five hundred pages, however, the *Neue Untersuchungen* is dominated by a single theme, that announced in Möhler's letters, namely, that Baur's views bear scant resemblance to those of the Reformers. On the very first page of the *Neue Untersuchungen,* under the heading "Schlimme Aussichten," one reads that Baur's *Genensatz* begins, not with original justice, but with original sin because Baur, unlike the faithful adherents of the three western confessions as well as the oriental churches, simply does not believe in original justice.[6] In his concluding remarks Möhler affirms, "I can therefore find ... only the differences between Baurism and Catholicism, nothing more."[7] Baurism scarcely befits a would-be Lutheran. Is it, in the end, that Herr Baur lacked the courage of his convictions? After but a faint-hearted defense of the old faith, "Herr Baur got some protective covering from the armory of the newer theology. His new attire, however, is related to orthodox Protestant theology as a Parisian frock coat of the year 1833 to the harness of a medieval knight."[8] Of course, Möhler continues, to be a knight in a frock coat is not all bad:

> It is beyond question that certain advantages attach to this new war matériel. Indeed, it exposes the noblest parts of the body; yet since it protects the back best of all and is very light, it is excellent for retreating and hurriedly making itself and its possessor scarce.[9]

The passage is characteristic. With a polemical irony reminiscent of Kierkegaard Möhler never misses a chance to lampoon what he considers the absurdity of this new and unlikely defense of classical Protestantism.[10] Even if this was the "dark side" of his nature expressing itself, the result is a theological treatise that is rather more entertaining than most.

[6]*NU*, p. 1.

[7]*NU*, p. 515.

[8]*NU*, p. 316.

[9]*Ibid.*

[10]This comparison is suggested in B. Hanssler, *Christliches Spektrum* (Frankfurt a/M, 1963), pp. 146-71. Hanssler's essay on Möhler is perhaps the best short discussion of the *totality* of Möhler's thought.

Although it is constantly being referred to, this single main theme receives explicit and extended attention in the third article of Chapter I.[11] The following pages will be devoted to the content of this article and will thus take up Möhler's extension of the controversy beyond the limits he had set for himself in the *Symbolik.* As he states in the preface to the third edition of the *Symbolik,* which was published in 1834,

> The very ponderous criticism of my *Symbolik* which in the meanwhile Professor Baur has put forth I will leave unnoticed in the present work, for the necessary discussions would occupy proportionally too great a space to find insertion either in the notes or in the text. I have therefore prepared to write a separate reply, which, please God, will soon be sent to the press.[12]

The present writer, it may be added, takes his justification for passing over the greater part of the *Neue Untersuchungen*—long discussions of specific dogmatic points—from Möhler's own remark to Adam Gengler, to wit, that Baur's work had "taken such a shape, that I see myself confirmed in my whole view of Lutheranism from having read it."[13] If with respect to the first task of symbolics Baur has said nothing new about Lutheranism, or Protestantism generally, with respect to the second task of symbolics he has said altogether too much that is new. It is time for us to examine more closely how grievously this sometime disciple of Schleiermacher has gone astray.

Möhler begins Chapter I, Article III, by noting that, paradoxical as this may seem, he and Baur are actually in fundamental agreement over how *systematically* to interpret and to structure the teachings of the Reformers. He immediately adds, of course, that if the Reformers had known that the *logical outcome* of their teachings was to be recent Protestantism they would promptly have disavowed them. Möhler's assertion, therefore, that Baur does not understand the actual, historical Reformers must be understood in connection with his other assertion to the effect that the Reformers did not fully understand themselves.

> I simply believed that I ought expressly to point out, by way of excusing the Reformers, that they were not conscious of the idea that formed the basis of

---

[11]*NU,* Secs. 25-31, pp. 121-74: "Herrn Baur's eigene auf die Reformatoren übertragene Ansicht von der Urgerechtigkeit, dem Ursprung des Bösen, und der Erbsunde mein Urtheil darüber."

[12]*S,* pp. 14f. (Robertson's translation, xxvii).

[13]A careful examination of the various editions of the *Symbolik,* the *Neue Untersuchungen,* and the *Gegensatz* makes it clear that neither Möhler nor Baur ever yielded a point to his opponent. Further editions simply brought further proof-texts and explanations, which are summarized in *MBC,* pp. 200-201, n. 1, and pp. 218-20, n. 2. An integral understanding of the Möhler-Baur exchange may thus be had by comparing the last editions of the *Symbolik* and the *Gegensatz,* together with the most relevant sections of Möhler's *Neue Untersuchungen* and Baur's "Erwiederung."

their whole system, for had they been conscious of it, I added, they would have rejected their system as unchristian. With respect to my interpretation of their doctrine Herr Baur now says, at least implicitly, that I am right, in that he himself adopts it; but he again says that I am right in that he praises precisely as in itself right and true [that is, the seeds of modern Protestantism] what I found to be objectionable therein. Indeed, he reprimands me with sharp words for having expressed myself censoriously and not unclearly gives me to understand that so miserable a creature as a Catholic must bend his knees before such men as the Reformers even when they are wrong.[14]

In a word, Möhler cannot win. Except, of course, that he thinks he can: he will draw attention to three points: (1) that the basic religious ideology incipiently advanced by the Reformers and developed further by Baur contradicts scripture; (2) that, questions of ideology aside, Baur has no *purely historical* justification for what he puts forward as Protestant dogma; and (3) that Baur's theories are inherently self-contradictory. Möhler discusses these three points in the context first of original sin and then of original justice.

Baur's conception of original sin is not to be found in the Old Testament.[15] That this is so does not, of course, trouble Baur, since, following Schleiermacher, he chooses not to regard the Old Testament as either formative or expressive of the Christian consciousness. But, argues Möhler, the Old Testament cannot be dismissed so lightly, "because the New Testament, with respect to the Old Testament view of the origin and idea of evil, altered nothing; rather, it pre-supposes this view throughout."[16] The witness of the Old Testament must therefore be heard.

From beginning to end the Old Testament understands the origin of evil in terms of the account in Genesis of Adam's fall. Whether or not the story of the fall is a myth is actually an irrelevant question; the important thing is that, myth or not, this story provides the conceptual framework within which the Old Testament deals with the origin of evil. In Genesis, then, we read that at the moment of their creation all God's creatures were good; "with the creation of finite beings ... evil was not already given."[17] In the case of man the first solicitation to evil came from a source outside man, "so that consequently evil was treated as the *counter-natural*."[18] Man's evildoing is thus presented as disobedience to God, "who ... instituted man's nature completely in harmony with his holy will."[19] Now, says Möhler,

---

[14]*NU,* p. 125. Sec. 25 is devoted to a short summary of Baur's views on the origin of evil, on original justice, and on original sin.

[15]*NU,* Sec. 26, pp. 127-35.

[16]*NU,* p. 128.

[17]*NU,* p. 129.

[18]*NU,* p. 130.

[19]*Ibid.*

if the sin of Adam is described as disobedience and the consequences of the same as punishment, it must be that the Hebrews considered man as endowed with freedom, as one in whose power it had been put to obey God and to deny him obedience—which, in any case, was already expressed by the fact of God's prohibition to man.[20]

Again, the facts of Adam's freedom and of the unnaturalness of his misuse of it are clearly expressed in Adam's shame after the fall. It is the foregoing conception of moral evil as rooted in human freedom that pervades the entire Old Testament. Even when God is said to harden men's hearts, the ultimate cause of this hardening is to be found in the human will, in men's turning away from God. Such was the common manner of expression of the Hebrew people: moral evil is man's fault; nowhere is this conception corrected in the New Testament.

Even considered quite apart from the Old Testament, however, the New Testament bears eloquent testimony to man's freedom and responsibility.[21] In the New Testament God is heard to forbid evildoing and to threaten punishment for it. And yet, if evil is implied in finitude, through creation itself, to forbid evil means, for God, nothing else but to lay down a constant protest against his own creation, incessantly to endeavor to annihilate it.[22] If God cannot repent of what he has done, however, man can; and yet, why should man be called upon to repent for his sins if he was never free to commit them? And what of the next life? In the New Testament the just man is promised heaven, where he will be free from absolutely all evil. And yet, "if the promise is well founded, and if, also, Herr Baur's doctrine is correct, just as this present life is limited today, heaven must be non-being."[23] If sin is simply finitude, all hope of a happy personal immortality is groundless. What of the existence of angels, beings finite and yet sinless? What, Schleiermacher notwithstanding, of hell? What, above all, of the incarnation itself?

Was not Christ also man? But how could he as such be without evil and sin, if the same lies in the idea of man as a finite being? In that holy scripture, therefore, presents Jesus Christ, the very Son of Man, as sinless, so, I should think, it is a doctrine wholly at variance with the whole bible that man as such is burdened with sin.[24]

Baur's conception of original sin is as alien to the Reformers as it is to the Bible they so prized. Throughout his discussion of Old and New Testament doctrines Möhler reminds the reader constantly that the Reformers—unlike Baur—firmly believed these doctrines. Baur's view "is based on the assumption

[20]NU, p. 131.
[21]NU, Sec. 27, pp. 135-44.
[22]NU, p. 136.
[23]NU, p. 137.
[24]NU, p. 139.

that Luther and his first pupils explained the Old Testament story of the fall allegorically."[25] But, replies Möhler, Luther understood it "*so literally* that not once is even a slight hint to be found" of an allegorical interpretation.[26] Luther's literalism went so far, for example, that he tried to determine what form the serpent had before the fatal scene at the tree: Did it go about upright "like a rooster"?[27] Baur's reading of Luther, Möhler continues, shows about as much historical understanding as a historian of steam engines' raising the question of "whether they were invented by Luther!"[28] It is clear, moreover, that when Baur tries to link his doctrine of the positive and the negative in man with Calvin's doctrine of the fall he breaks all the laws of historical understanding and historiography—and not infrequently comes up with something quite laughable. Calvin did not teach that God created man partially evil, or that finitude is to be understood as evil. Even if Calvin's own doctrine involved him in self-contradiction, one is still not justified in attributing doctrines to him that were not his own.

Not only is Baur a bad historian. He is also a bad logician, and his theories, like Calvin's, are grossly wanting in internal coherence.[29] Why, in the first place, to use Baur's expression, must the "positive" in man always be accompanied by the "negative"? "This assertion," says Möhler, "is drawn from common empiricism and has no deeper basis for itself, for from the fact that we now see so many good things develop only through opposition to evil, it by no means follows that good does not *at all* develop without evil, or indeed, that without evil good cannot be."[30] A biblical theologian is clearly bound to affirm that, whatever man's present state, in the beginning there was no evil; moreover, the biblical theologian can never become entangled in the shallow empiricism which states that whatever lies outside our experience must remain forever unknown to us, that of it we cannot make for ourselves a clear *Vorstellung*. Is not evil, in addition, always spoken of in the fashion of good? If evil, properly speaking, is nothing, must one not already have a concept of good or of something good in order to be able to speak of evil? Baur's form of arguing is circular: If we ask Baur why there is evil in the world, he replies that it cannot be otherwise; yet if we ask him why it cannot be otherwise, he replies that this is the way the world is. True, without revelation we could not account satisfactorily for the origin of evil. Nevertheless, to allegorize the revealed account of the origin of evil is, in terms of that account, ultimately, "to make the devil a condition   for the existence of God."[31]

[25]*NU*, p. 145.

[26]*Ibid.*

[27]Möhler, *ibid.*, is obviously pleased that Luther said this, but he does not say where.

[28]*NU*, p. 146, Sec. 28, pp. 145-47.

[29]*NU*, Sec. 129, pp. 147-59.

[30]*NU*, p. 147.

[31]*NU*, p. 148.

Whereas traditional theology had room for *both* a doctrine of creation *and* a doctrine of the fall, Baur's theology treats the doctrine of the fall as a *substitute* for that of creation. The anthropomorphism of a divine act of creation is, in narrative form, simply a presentation of the more philosophical doctrine of the origin of evil and finitude through a divine self-limitation. Yet, Möhler argues, if at times the creation story seems somewhat naive, the doctrine of divine self-limitation is even more naive; in fact, it is no more than a verbal fiction.

> If the negative is to be treated as the limit which the creative activity sets for itself in the production of the creature, and if the creature itself is possible only through this limitation, how can this limitation be at once a deterioration of the creature or necessarily result in such a deterioration, since it is precisely through this limitation that the creature came to be in the first place? If the limit belongs to the nature of the creature in the sense that without limitation its existence is quite impossible, so everything that pertains to this limitation . . . is not at all a deterioration of its nature but is rather entirely in order . . . .[32]

Baur cannot have it both ways. If evil is finitude, then creatures cannot have any kind of distinct existence or intelligibility within the divine ground: if God limits himself, he must limit himself to something determinate, and therefore finite. But if finitude can in any way be predicated of God, then God himself, and not only the creature, is evil. On the other hand, if by some kind of metaphysical judo the creature in some manner attains existence outside the divine ground, it is difficult to see why limitation must necessarily be conceived as evil; after all, the creature is simply the term of a presumably holy divine purpose. In short, talk about a divine self-limitation that results in a limited, and therefore evil, creature is simply a screen of verbiage that does not even successfully conceal the metaphysical embarrassment behind it.

It must also be pointed out that the human consciousness does not at all spontaneously recognize finitude as evil, or in human terms, sin. Baur's would-be empiricism cannot bear even empirical scrutiny. What does consciousness tell us of our relationship to God, not, for the moment, as moral agents, but simply as human beings? "From limitedness results only that the creature cannot exceed a certain measure of love for God or ambition against him or the good generally; how is it supposed to come about that precisely *because* the creature is finite it acts *against* God himself . . . ?"[33] It is simply untrue to experience and downright illogical to pass "from limited being to moral perversion."[34] Physical and moral evil are different orders of being and language. Moral evil is something that a physically good creature, by reason of its freedom, is able to do. By transmuting what metaphysics and consciousness testify to be moral evil into purely

[32]*NU*, p. 149.

[33]*NU*, p. 150.

[34]*NU*, p. 151.

physical evil, Baur's theory paradoxically makes real *moral good* inconceivable.

Baur has nevertheless argued that the fall is man's fault. Möhler once again confesses his inability to see how a state that is necessarily bound "with the eternal idea" of man can be experienced or conceptualized as man's fault.[35] This is particularly difficult where the system of thought in question also denies man's freedom of choice; without the capability of choosing between alternatives how could man ever commit what could be described as a *fault*? In terms of biblical theology Baur faces an irresolvable dilemma: He must make up his mind either to say that sin is not a movement of the will against God—and thereby cease to be a biblically-oriented theologian, or, if he does not give up the biblical idea of sin, to say that even though God does everything, *we* are still able to rebel against him. To escape from the dilemma, as Baur attempts to do, with the assertion that evil is evil only from man's point of view, not from God's, has, once again, the effect of making God diabolic. Do murders really serve God's purpose? The thought is repugnant to our moral feelings, and yet, has conscience itself been given to us by an evil God? What could we say to such a being, asks Möhler, except, "We suspected you all along, because you constantly embittered with an inner snakebite so many of the joys of life"?[36]

From what Baur says of the origin of evil and sin one can conclude only that he is a pantheist, that for him

> the relationship of God to the world is to be set down as that of the substance of nature to its individual productions, so that, quite simply, we are divine individuals. Through the differentiation of the divine essence the universe comes into being, and we are the very creative power of God, in so far as it manifests itself in single limited appearances.[37]

Needless to say—with the possible exception of Zwingli—the Reformers would have abhorred Baur's denial of the doctrine of creation. On this point they agreed perfectly with their Catholic adversaries, even if subsequently the Catholics looked to man and the Protestants to God as the ultimate cause of the fall. Even if he does not fully realize it—for he disavows it—Baur is a pantheist, not a Protestant.

Turning now to Baur's conception of original justice, Möhler finds that here again Baur offers but a caricature of classical Protestantism.[38] Luther, it is true, taught that original justice was an essential element of Adam's nature. Luther, however, went on to teach that Adam lost this original justice. Baur does not agree: "According to his theory of Protestantism man is *essentially* just and therefore indelibly so."[39] Baur sees "the whole history of mankind and of the individual

---

[35]*Ibid.*

[36]*NU*, p. 154.

[37]*NU*, p. 156.

[38]*NU*, Sec. 30, pp. 159-71.

[39]*NU*, p. 159.

only as a dynamic development of those powers that are in the strictest sense man's own and that constitute his essence."[40] Christ is the highest point of this evolutionary process. And yet, Möhler asks, why cannot one say that Adam, not Christ, is the high point, and that, consequently the hypothesis of evolution is quite gratuitous, there being no evolution at all? After all, "no God could develop out of mankind if mankind were not of divine being itself, if God had not already been in it from the beginning, indeed, if mankind were not itself God."[41] Or, assuming the hypothesis of evolution, why cannot one assume that man will evolve beyond Christ? To mix the natural and the supernatural as Baur does is not Christian. "Schleiermacher, whose opinions, without a sharp exam- ination, Herr Baur makes his own," treats the God-man relationship as one of *natura naturans* to *natura naturata*.[42] Schleiermacher? "One need only trace these formulae to their origin in order to decipher their meaning."[43] And their origin lies in Schelling's "immature period." In his. *Vorlesungen über die Methode des akademischen Studiums* Schelling stated that the incarnation is to be understood as the summit, and therefore, the beginning, or principle, of the process because the infinite was manifested better in Christ than in anyone else. Schelling then is ultimately to blame—except that, unlike Schleiermacher and Baur, he has subsequently had the good sense to abandon such a position.[44] Protestant though he may be, Schelling is much too sensitive to the myriad richness and depth of man's religiosity. But Baur wants to foist upon the Reformers a theology that has already been discarded by its true originator.

Once the incarnation is treated, not as the providential divine means for the restoration of man's original justice, but as a mythological presentation of the dignity of man, there is not very much left of Christianity. The doctrine of the trinity is obviously ruled out. So also are the doctrines of the atonement, of the forgiveness of sin, and of regeneration. It becomes inconceivable how Christian- ity could become a scandal to the world, except, Möhler suggests, that good pagans might be impelled to ask, "Is it a sin to have been a child and a youth?"[45] Needless to add, all those doctrines upon which the Reformers lavished so much attention have completely vanished. In this new Christianity we no longer worry about sin and grace; no—"little gods that we all are, as we fall on our knees before Christ and honor in him only our own divine being, the god in our very selves satisfies all our needs and every desire."[46] It is absurd,

[40]*NU*, p. 160.

[41]*NU*, pp. 160f.

[42]*NU*, p. 161.

[43]*NU*, p. 162.

[44]The passage Möhler quotes is to be found in *Schellings Werke*, ed. M. Schroter, III (Munich, 1927), 319f.

[45]*NU*, p. 164.

[46]*NU*, p. 168.

then, to consider such views Protestant. Suppose Baur were to send a statement of his views, with a request for signatures of approval, to all the German faculties of Protestant theology. How many signatures would he get? From the Protestant faculty of Tübingen, Möhler suggests, he would get but one!

Suppose, however, that Baur were to agree that his presentation of the doctrines of original justice and original sin does not correspond with historical Protestantism.[47] Could he not still argue that, despite some infelicities of presentation, perhaps, it still translates better than any other doctrinal system currently available the immediate data of the Christian consciousness at its current state of development? Möhler's reply is a categorical No! In other words, not only are Baur's conceptions of the various individual doctrines unacceptable—so is his basic methodological principle.

Christianity, as the whole foregoing argument has undertaken to demonstrate, is that religion in which forgiveness of sin comes to man from the transcendent God whom he has offended. It should be clear, then, that "Christianity, as that which it claims to be, can be adhered to . . . only on the basis of freedom."[48] Even Baur appears to admit that man thinks himself to have the power of free choice. For Möhler the *consciousness* of freedom is so evidently present as to be entirely beyond question. Schleiermacher's feeling of absolute dependence may have some truth to it; but if the absoluteness of absolute dependence is taken to mean that man has no freedom of choice, Möhler cannot accept it; he cannot conceive, he says, "that a manner of religious thinking that has the moral consciousness against it" can be *the* "authentic religious" manner of thinking.[49] Even if the feeling of absolute dependence satisfies the religious aspirations of man, religion must not and need not be sacrificed to man's moral consciousness. And man's moral consciousness cannot be taken to be, as Baur would have it, a specification of a more basic intuition or consciousness. Were this the case, Christianity as a dispensation of real forgiveness for real sins would be rendered absurd and vain; sins, in this case, would not proceed from the center of man's personality.

It is no wonder, then, as Möhler argues in the conclusion to the whole of the *Neue Untersuchungen,* that Schleiermacher's and Baur's Christian consciousness is unable to authenticate itself as Christian.[50] How does the Christian consciousness come to know itself as Christian? Baur would doubtless reply, "It has its certitude in itself." He would "without doubt base himself on the freedom of belief and knowledge" that he believes to exist in Protestantism.[51] He would have to, remarks Möhler, for there is nothing left for consciousness to

[47]*NU,* Sec. 31, pp. 171-73.

[48]*NU,* p. 172.

[49]*NU,* p. 173.

[50]*NU,* pp. 509-41.

[51]*NU,* pp. 516f.

rest on but itself; scripture as interpreted by living tradition has been made subordinate to consciousness. When such is the case, however, a man's consciousness—since it is but his consciousness of himself—will normally only tell him that in some sense he is what he ought to be; nothing can come in from the outside to challenge him. Such is plainly the case, for example, among those Jews, Muslims, and heathens that happen to live under Christian rule and influence.

Even if it be granted, as it surely may, that man's consciousness cries out for the forgiveness of sin, this fact does not serve to release consciousness from itself. Rather, a consciousness of sin that is only that and no more tends to exclude the only source of forgiveness:

> If Herr Baur conceives sin as being only personal and individual, only as the personal deed of each man, so can he conceive redemption only in a purely personal manner, only as the personal deed of each single individual; if to him the first Adam is only the type of man as falling because he is a finite being, so can the second Adam be for him only the type of the lifting up from the fall of the being of man, which being, in its very finitude, is still infinite; as man must, as flesh, . . . fall, so must he, as spirit, . . . lift himself up from the fall.[52]

The ultimate tragedy of consciousness left to itself is that it must posit an ideal, imaginary counterfeit of what it needs. It must posit, as historical, a historical redeemer without being able to come into any sort of vital contact with him. The testimony of the authentic Christian consciousness is altogether different. The consciousness of a real Christian—let us say it quite frankly, of the Catholic Christian who reaches the historical Christ in and through the historical church—sets no high value on solitary self-reliance. His consciousness "tells him that he . . . can attain to rest and peace with God only from free grace, not through progressive natural development."[53] If more carefully examined, therefore, the Christian consciousness itself rises up against "Baurism." Its inmost desire is for free forgiveness, freely given by God, for what it has freely done wrong. That ultimate freedom of the Christian, namely to rest in absolute dependence upon God, is founded on man's freedom of choice. Therefore, concludes Möhler, "There must be a dogma which corresponds in like manner to both man's religious and moral needs: we honor it in Catholicism."[54]

Baur's "Erwiederung"

Möhler's *Neue Untersuchungen* appeared in June, 1834. Baur fought back almost immediately; in the third number of the *Tübinger Zeitschrift für*

[52]*NU*; p. 526.

[53]*NU*, p. 530.

[54]*NU*, p. 175.

Theologie for the same year there appeared the one-hundred-twenty-odd pages of Baur's "Erwiederung auf Herrn Dr. Möhler's neueste Polemik."

Indeed, Baur *fought* back. If Möhler moved from scholarly seriousness to a teasing irony under the pressure of what he took to be personal attacks from Baur, the latter, under what he took to be similar treatment, moved from seriousness to righteous wrath. Möhler, we are told, was an elegant and witty man.[55] Baur was a shy sort of person, a man perhaps not without a touch of professorial primness.[56] The "Erwiederung" eloquently testifies to Baur's embarrassment at being lampooned and not being able or willing to reply in kind. He quotes in full, for example, the passage about the knight in the frock coat, and then adds, "I have set down this passage here only for this reason, that I find the best answer to it to be that I myself would wish it the greatest possible publicity."[57] One wonders whether, for Baur at least, the best answer would have been to avoid answering. . . .

In his biographical sketch of Baur, Eduard Zeller, Baur's son-in-law, remarks that the content of the "Erwiederung" was largely incorporated into the second edition of the *Gegensatz,* which was published in 1836.[58] On the whole, Zeller is right, but two qualifications are in order. The first is that the "Erwiederung" so abounds in outraged rhetorical questions and the like that the "Erwiederung" contains very little that is not to be found in the *first* edition of the *Gegensatz!* Again and again Baur points out that since Möhler is still entangled in the same misconceptions, there is little that he, Baur, can do to alter the situation. The relatively few, mostly verbal clarifications that Baur does attempt have, for simplicity's sake, been placed in the notes to Chapter III of the present study, and need not be discussed more at length here. Secondly, however, Zeller's brief general description of the "Erwiederung" must also be qualified by noting that there is a certain amount of interesting material in the "Erwiederung" that is not to be found in either edition of the *Gegensatz.* After taking up in turn the sixteenth-century Protestant positions on original justice and original sin, justification, the sacraments, and the church, Baur concludes with a consideration—roughly the last twenty pages of the article—of the relationship between sixteenth and nineteenth-century Protestantism.[59] In these pages Baur replies to

[55]See, e.g., F. X. Reithmayr's "Lebensskizze" in *S*-II, p. 134.

[56]See, e.g., Hodgson, *op. cit.,* pp. 8 and 34. A gentle demythologizing of the admiring portraiture alluded to in this and the preceding note—coupled with an extended reading of Möhler's and Baur's writings—leaves one with a not inconsiderable sense of acquaintance with them as men. Good and interesting men.

[57]*E*, p. 205.

[58]Eduard Zeller, "Ferdinand Christian Baur," in *Vorträge und Abhandlungen geschichtlichen Inhalts* (Leipzig, 1875), p. 431n. This study first appeared shortly after Baur's death (in 1861) in the *Preussische Jahrbücher.* Losch, *Gengler,* p. 120, n. 4, repeats Zeller's observation.

[59]*E*, pp. 226-48.

the charges made by Möhler in Chapter I, Article III, and in the Conclusion of the *Neue Untersuchungen,* and summarized in the first section of the present chapter. Although Baur does not in these pages alter his opinions, he still presents them in a manner sufficiently different from what he had thus far written to warrant the following summary.

Baur states that he conceives his task as a symbolical controversialist to be a twofold undertaking. In the first place he is called upon to demonstrate that sixteenth-century Protestantism is in no way "without sense and reason," as Möhler would have it, but is actually superior to Catholicism in its ability to satisfy man's religious as well as his moral aspirations. His task does not end here, however, for the very nature of Protestantism demands that he also discuss the relationship between the Protestantism of the sixteenth and that of the nineteenth century. Unlike Catholicism, Protestantism is not bound to the mere language of symbolical books or to the pronouncements of human authorities. It is free and developmental in nature. Therefore, continues Baur,

> I have . . . not limited my defense of the Protestant doctrinal idea to the bare letter of our symbols, but . . . have throughout also directed my view beyond the symbols and treated Protestant theology as a science understood to be in constant development and formation. On this account I have so expressed those views and convictions which I as a theologian of the nineteenth century confess, and do not hesitate to confess publicly, as to indicate throughout their connection with our symbolical doctrinal concept and their point of departure within it . . . .[60]

The legitimacy of Baur's method of discussing Protestantism is therefore rooted in the evolutionary character of Protestantism. Hence the objection that Baur's or anyone else's nineteenth-century Protestantism is different from that of the sixteenth century is really irrelevant. If Protestantism is evolutionary, nineteenth-century Protestantism *must* differ from that of the sixteenth century; and if it did not differ from the latter partially, paradoxically, perhaps, it would differ from it *completely.* He who would evaluate the work of a given nineteenth-century Protestant theologian is not, therefore, to trouble himself over whether this theologian's work corresponds to some supratemporal, static norm; he is rather to investigate the extent to which this theologian's work responds, in the spirit of Protestantism, to the nineteenth-century religious situation. Just as the work of the Reformers met the needs of their time, so must that of modern theologians meet those of today.

It may appear that Baur is simply saying that to be right or to be opportune is to be Protestant, to be in conformity with the Reformers. Such is not the case. What Baur has in mind is that in the Reformation western man's religious development took a decisive step forward; by beginning, at least, to direct man's attention away from externals and inward toward his own self-consciousness, the

Reformers established the pattern to which authentic religiosity had thereafter to conform. Man's religious self-consciousness has evolved: to recognize this fact, in a word, to be Protestant, is therefore the way to be right and opportune about religious truth. Protestantism is not absolute truth; what it is—and this is of crucial import—is the only way in which modern man can become receptive to absolute religious truth. When, therefore, the Catholic insists on the necessity of ecclesiastical authority as the means of man's appropriation of religious truth, what is the Protestant to reply? When the Catholic repeats the position of sixteenth-century Catholicism on the necessity of hierarchical tradition, the only really appropriate Protestant reply is to emphasize the underlying methodological continuity of past and present Protestant thought.

Catholicism brings the divine into too low a station. In Protestantism, on the contrary, it is assumed that God will do his part by maintaining in constancy the basic referent of Christian dogmatics; man does not have to do that, but rather only to remain open to divine truth, to be aware that it is in his very consciousness, untrammeled by authoritarian restrictions, that God speaks to him. Provided God does his part, for the modern theologian to insist on inwardness in no sense implies a denial of traditional doctrines, but, if anything, a deepening of them. Baur's point is thus that for him to treat Protestant theology as a science in constant development in no sense leads him into interesting, perhaps, but pointless theological *obiter dicta*. Moreover, so little is it an indication that he is ignorant of the Reformers' teaching that the opposite is the case; they were champions of freedom of belief and thought, and Baur, not his adversary, has understook what the Reformers were about. Either, as is lamentably the case in Catholicism, man himself must attempt to guarantee the transmission of religious truth, or, as in Protestantism, man must, at every step of his ethico-religious evolution, remain open to the influence of the divine guarantor. For Baur, at least, Protestantism is infinitely to be preferred as an alternative. In terms, now, not of static, supra-temporal creedal statements, but of the development of doctrine, such is what the *sola fide* of Protestantism necessarily means.

The root of the problem of the origin of evil is the problem of the meaning of human freedom. Evil, for man, originated in a human act: was man, ultimately, free or determined so to act? As is entirely consistent with his understanding of Protestantism, Baur insists that his view of the problem of freedom "is as old as Protestantism, and is founded on the same principles by Schleiermacher as by Luther and Calvin."[61] In a rather interesting piece of reasoning Baur sets forth *the* Protestant view of freedom:

> Indeed, the question is simply this: If Protestant doctrine on one hand denies any power for good to man for himself, and on the other hand derives all true good from divine activity, we have here the premises of a view that can in no way be reconciled with the usual concept of freedom.[62]

[61]*E*, p. 227.
[62]*Ibid.*

The usual, in the sense of both frequently encountered and imperfectly analyzed, concept of freedom is freedom of choice, *liberum arbitrium*. Baur continues:

> If man is not free in the usual sense, if thus good is not his own doing but only the effect of grace, so also evil is not his own doing, because only that can be considered a will-act in the proper sense that proceeds from freedom as the capacity of choice between good and evil. Since, however, the existence of evil cannot be denied, there remain only these alternatives: either God is the author, not only of good, but also of evil—which immediately contradicts the concept of God; or evil is not to be traced to the same causality as good—that is, evil is not something positive, but, as such, it is the negation of good.[63]

It is not his intention, Baur notes, to work out this chain of reasoning in the greatest possible detail. It suffices to bear in mind that the whole argument rests on presuppositions "which have their truth in themselves, for who would deny that God is absolute causality?"[64] But if God is absolute causality, and God can only cause good, then evil simply must not exist. To speak of evil, in other words, is to use a linguistic model borrowed from speech about good, and therefore evil as such does not exist. Ultimately, then, man causes neither good nor evil. The existence of evil becomes a problem because man often believes himself to possess the freedom to cause it; the solution to both these problems— evil and freedom— is to demolish the two illusions—evil and freedom—that cause them.

The defenders of both a superficial, purely empirical understanding of freedom and a superficial reading of the New Testament cannot really make a very good case for their opinions. Is it true that for God to forbid evildoing is, in effect, for him to protest against his own creation? Not at all, replies Baur. Freedom in the sense of *liberum arbitrium* can exist, if it exists at all, only in the finite world; in God freedom and necessity are one. A finite freedom, however, that would be somehow prevented from sometimes choosing evil would not really be freedom at all, at least not in the sense of *liberum arbitrium*. Hence, paradoxically, "also according to this view of freedom, to forbid evil means nothing else than to annihilate the conditions of creation and to lay down a protest against the existence of the world."[65] One cannot avoid thinking, then, that no matter how one conceives human freedom, a divine prohibition of evil, if taken quite literally, is a self-contradictory divine protest against creation. In a word, if God does not want sin, he should not have given man such a freedom as would inevitably lead to sin. Nothing is to be gained, therefore, by substituting a problematic literal reading of scripture for what was misunderstood to be a problematic figurative reading.

Similar difficulties attach to an unduly literal reading of scriptural appeals

[63]*E*, p. 228.
[64]*Ibid.*
[65]*E*, p. 229.

for repentance for sin, and scriptural proclamations of the forgiveness of sin. Möhler argues that if sin is simply the divinely ardained limitation of man's being, presumably man's being freed from sin, if not here, at least in heaven, means really that man ceases to exist, that the boundaries that define his being simply fall away. This is nonsense, counters Baur, for if one properly understands what "sin" means, the whole problem, as already noted, is seen to be illusory:

> With regard to the assertion that the negative view of evil is not founded on anything biblical, . . . it is easy to see that the whole weight of this objection rests only on the reading given to *sin*. If one calls *sin* all that simply which constitutes the distinction between creator and creature, it is certainly right that sin ceases no less than can the distinction between creator and creature; one must simply be reasonable enough to admit that nothing is hereby stated except what can in no case be denied, that, so long as man is man, the limit can never be thought away which separates him from the creator, the absolute god.[66]

To be finite, therefore, is to be "evil," a "sinner":

> In this sense the highest created spirit can no more be thought of without a minimum of sin than the most depraved of the fallen spirits without a minimum of good, because that it is a spirit is, as real, something good.[67]

Even in the case of Christ must evil be present, not grossly, of course, but as a minimum tending to vanish but never vanishing. For Christ did have freedom, and yet, "what is freedom, insofar as it is not, as in God, one with necessity, other than the possibility of evil, and thus already a minimum of evil?"[68] Like any man Christ had the experience of the freedom of choice, of separation from the absolute good. To take away Christ's experience is to deny his humanity, just as to take away his insight into the real nature of things is to deny the presence of the divine in him.

Baur now takes up Möhler's objections to his conception of original justice.[69] Möhler, it will be recalled, found fault with Baur's appropriation of Schleiermacher's less than total distinction between the natural, fallen man in need of redemption and the supernatural heights from which he has fallen and supernatural means by which he is to regain his former state. Now why, asks Baur, does Möhler so object to Schleiermacher? In the *Symbolik* has not Möhler himself conceded Baur's whole case? Baur quotes the following passage in extra-large print: "WITH ALL HIS DEVIATIONS ON PARTICULAR POINTS, SCHLEIERMACHER IS, IN MY OPINION, THE ONLY GENUINE DISCIPLE

[66]*E*, p. 231.
[67]*E*, pp. 231f.
[68]*E*, p. 232.
[69]*E*, p. 237.

OF THE REFORMERS."[70] If this is what Möhler really thinks, why is he so disturbed? True, absolute supernaturalism is the basis of Catholicism, but is not Schleiermacher in accord with right reason in insisting that there must be an "inner, essential relatedness of the human spirit to God as the absolute spirit," a "receptivity and an inner point of contact for Christianity"?[71] Moreover, despite Möhler's insistence that the Reformers thought of man as a brute beast, is not the truth rather that they denied, not man's reason without qualification, but only the higher exercise of it? Möhler objects, not to the truth of the situation, but only to evils of his own devising.

Why has Möhler done this? Baur notes that Möhler's *Neue Untersuchungen* has the character of a personal attack on him, and yet, he feels, his person is not primarily the subject of Möhler's ironic misrepresentations.[72] No, it is every right-thinking Protestant, it is Protestantism itself. As Möhler himself recognizes in the *Symbolik,* Protestantism is experiencing a new vitality, in part, at least "through the favor of one of the most influential ministries of Germany." In the face of the new power of Protestantism Catholics feel that they are called upon to revive the old hatred. They feel threatened, or, perhaps, envy is the root of their "opposition against the noble sentiments with which an enlightened, genuinely Evangelical government makes its own the cause of the Evangelical Church."[73]

Möhler and Catholics like him are disturbers of the peace. Let them reconsider the gravity of what they are doing. How many really enlightened Catholics would agree to Möhler's course? Not many, thinks Baur:

> I am convinced that if signatures approving such an undertaking were to be collected, even among Herr Möhler's own faculty colleagues—especially when they considered how they would set themselves in opposition to the principles of a government that protects with watchful care, for the best interests of the state, the sciences, and all society, the peaceful living together of the two confessions—*not one signature* could be obtained.[74]

For his part, adds Baur, he takes leave of his adversary with the wish "never again to have to meet him on the battleground of this so unpleasant controversy."[75]

---

[70]*E,* p. 238.

[71]*E,* p. 239.

[72]*E,* pp. 244-48.

[73]*E,* p. 247.

[74]*E,* p. 248.

[75]*Ibid.*

Baur's Die christliche Gnosis

Nothing warms the heart of a controversialist so much as having the last word. At any rate, inasmuch as Möhler had, in the course of 1835, replied to Baur's "Erwiederung" with a second, improved edition of his *Neue Untersuchungen,* Baur felt called upon to reply to these *new* new investigations with a second, improved edition of his *Der Gegensatz.* This he did in the course of 1836. And, as we shall see, he thereby had the last word.

As has already been pointed out, however, these two second editions differ but slightly from the first editions of the works in question; above all, in no case did the authors retract in their second editions opinions they had advanced in their first. Rather, therefore, than exhaustively to examine these reissues, it is of much more importance, for understanding the Möhler-Baur controversy as a whole, to take a careful look at a work with which Baur appears to have been occupied even while preparing his "Erwiederung" and the second edition of his *Gegensatz,* namely, his *Die christliche Gnosis, oder die christliche Religionsphilosophie in ihrer geschichtlichen Entwicklung.*[76]

To the attentive reader Baur's "Erwiederung" and *Gegensatz* raise an interesting, if also rather amusing question. Where, *really,* did Baur get his understanding of Protestant dogmatics? Baur often presents Schleiermacher's opinions. But is Schleiermacher his only mentor? Clearly not. Baur even more often takes positions that can only with extreme difficulty be ascribed to Schleiermacher, positions, however, that any reader familiar with Hegel's writings on religion will readily recognize as paraphrases of the latter's texts.[77] Nevertheless, whereas Baur often mentions Schleiermacher by name, he rarely mentions Hegel. Oddly, his longest reference to Hegel occurs in his basically favorable report on what recent *Catholic* Hegelians (like Anton Günther) are doing. One can only conclude that when writing expressly on Protestant dogmatics, Baur cautiously omits some obvious footnotes so as not to alarm those who have heard that Hegel is an irreligious rationalist but have never read him! When writing on Christian gnosis, that is to say, on the philosophy of religion, Baur shows no such hesitation. With but trifling qualifications, Baur seems to be saying, Hegel is the best philosopher of religion to date, *precisely because Hegel's philosophy of religion is able to absorb dogmatics,* able to render dogmatics luminous with reason even while avoiding the extremes of Catholicism's externalism and Schleiermacher's subjectivism. In the *Christliche Gnosis,* then, we find a formal statement of the Hegelian outlook which, half explicitly, half implicitly, had been put forth in the "Erwiederung" and the *Gegensatz.*

---

[76](Tübingen: C. F. Oslander, 1835; repr. Darmstadt: Wissenschaftliche Buchgesellschaft, 1967).

[77]See, e.g., G. W. F. Hegel, *The Phenomenology of Mind,* tr. J. Baillie (New York 1967), pp. 609f.

The text of *Die christliche Gnosis* runs to seven-hundred-odd pages. Baur first discusses the concept and the origin of gnosticism. He then takes up the principal forms of early gnosticism, classifying them according to how they conceive the relationship among heathenism, Judaism, and Christianity. Next he considers the struggle between gnosticism, on the one hand, and neoplatonism and so-called "orthodoxy" on the other. Finally he turns to "The Old Gnosis and the Newer Philosophy of Religion," in which last part of his treatise he examines the religious thought of Böhme, Schelling, Schleiermacher, and Hegel. It is Baur's treatment of Hegel, Chapter IV, Section 4 of *Gnosis*, that is chiefly of interest here.[78]

Baur, of course, must immediately answer, at least in a provisory manner, the question of why he includes Böhme and the other modern "gnostics" in what one would have expected to be a study of the adversaries of the orthodox church fathers. Baur answers the question by advancing a hypothetical delineation of "gnosis": in the body of the work he will show how this initial hypothesis is in fact verified, how it is, in a word, the very concept of Christian gnosis.[79] In Chapter I, Section 1, then, Baur begins by noting that, whatever it is, gnosis has to do with religion. Gnosis, however, does not revolve around an abstract idea of religion; rather it attempts to determine the relationship of various historical manifestations of religion, namely, of Christianity and the various forms of heathenism and Judaism that were contemporary with the beginnings of Christianity.[80] Baur emphasizes that gnosis is not simply philosophy; it always deals with historical religions. But gnosis is not simply the history of religions either.

> Gnosis, namely, is history of religion only insofar as it is at the same time philosophy of religion, and the characteristic manner in which these two elements and directions, the historical and the philosophical, have mutually penetrated one another and been bound into one whole gives us the proper concept of its essence.[81]

The task of the philosophical element of gnosis is to reflect on what the historical element reports, to discover, by so doing, that the various forms of historical religion are parts of a single whole, a whole "in which one and the same living idea, in its concrete configuration, progresses through a series of forms and levels of development."[82] "All religions," Baur continues,

> are one in the idea of religion; they are related to it as the appearance and

[78]*Gnosis*, pp. 668-735.

[79]*Ibid.*, pp. 10-36.

[80]*Ibid.*, pp. 18ff.

[81]*Ibid.*, p. 21.

[82]*Ibid.*

form to the essence, the concrete to the abstract, the mediating to the
immediate. The whole of the history of religion [in the sense of religious
events] is nothing else but the living, self-unfolding and progressing, and, as a
result, self-realizing concept of religion . . . .[83]

But, one might inquire, where is this idea of religion? Or better, who has it?
Or better still, who *is* it? The answer, naturally, is God. The essence of religion
lies in deity itself: God is the abstract (in the sense of pregnant but undeter-
mined plenitude), the immediate, that which in and through religion men strive
to grasp, to conceive. It is not improper to say that religion is God reaching out
of and being united with God. When gnosis is said to deal with the various
historical religions, what is meant but that it deals with their content? Thus, for
gnosis, says Baur, "the idea of religion immediately collapses into one unity with
that which it has as its essential and necessary content, the idea of deity."[84]
Thus it comes about that when gnosis is said to involve philosophic reflection on
the historical events of religion, much more is being said than first appeared to
be the case. It is hardly a question here of mere generalizations about previously
"bracketed" phenomena! In and through the study of religious-historical
phenomena gnosis is—quite self-consciously—the study of God. For Christian
gnosis

the history of religion is not merely the history of divine revelations; rather are
these revelations at the same time the process of development in which the
eternal essence of the deity itself goes out of itself, manifests itself in a finite
world, and alienates itself from itself, in order through this manifestation and
self-alienation to turn back to eternal unity with itself.[85]

Gnosis has ever evoked lively interest, and it is easy to see why. It is man's
attempt to grasp what the divine life is, to reflect lovingly the loving self-
reflection of God. As such, therefore, gnosis is not confined to any one human
era, even if the term gnosis often has a more restricted meaning. As Baur has it,

This remarkable attempt to comprehend nature and history, the whole course
of the world with all that it includes, as the series of moments in which the
absolute spirit objectifies itself and mediates itself with itself is even the more
remarkable in that gnosis in this sense has nothing more related and analogous
in the whole history of philosophical and theological speculation than the
most recent philosophy of religion.[86]

Well, then, what about modern philosophy of religion? In Chapter IV of *Die
christliche Gnosis* Baur gives detailed descriptions of the religious thought of

[83]*Ibid.*
[84]*Ibid.*, p. 22.
[85]*Ibid.*
[86]*Ibid.*, p. 24.

Böhme, Schelling, Schleiermacher, and Hegel, undertaking throughout to point out the similarities between these men's systems and different forms of patristic gnosticism. (It may be noted in passing that, regarding the modern term of the comparison, these descriptions by Baur are—quite simply—masterful, rarely equalled in clairvoyance.) With respect to Böhme and Schelling, despite the enormous importance of these men, Baur concludes that philosophy of religion has not quite come into its own: Böhme and Schelling are still too much under the domination of imaginative, mythic fancy.[87] With respect to Schleiermacher—somewhat surprisingly, considering that Schleiermacher is *never* adversely criticized in the "Erwiederung" and the *Gegensatz*—Baur repeats what he said in the above-mentioned lecture of 1828.

Schleiermacher's problem is that he is locked within subjectivity. "So long," notes Baur,

> as self-consciousness has not expanded itself into a general world-consciousness, the utterances of religious life can express absolute dependence only with respect to a single finite being, not, however, with respect to the whole world—and even this feeling of absolute dependence lacks the outward expansion that it has to have if the absolute is really to be that which absolutely determines.[88]

Schleiermacher's non-achievement as a philosopher of religion can be aptly summed up by saying that Schleiermacher has *regressed* into Kantianism. Or rather, Schleiermacher's "mystical darkness" can actually be rendered more comprehensible by Kant's rational clarity.[89] What lies beyond consciousness, that upon which man is unconditionally dependent, is for both Kant and Schleiermacher a *noumenon*; what lies within consciousness is subjectivity gone wild:

> The standpoint of Kant and Schleiermacher is, in a word, the same standpoint of subjectivity, in which, as Hegel characterizes this standpoint, "all objective content vanishes, only what is posited by me avails, and I alone am the positive, the real; . . . in this contentless standpoint no religion at all is possible . . . ."[90]

The basic difference between Schleiermacher and Hegel is that whereas Schleiermacher insists that philosophy is a kind of separate province that has nothing in particular to do with religion, Hegel shows how philosophy helps

---

[87]*Ibid.*, pp. 611 and 626.

[88]*Ibid.*, pp. 634f. An analogous problem occurs with Schleiermacher's Christology: "The whole doctrine of the person of Christ is also . . . primarily only a description of a certain human state, that, namely, of redemption; and the redeemer is nothing else but the idea of redemption as thought out in personal terms . . . ." *Ibid.*, p. 652.

[89]*Ibid.*, p. 660.

[90]*Ibid.*, pp. 666f.

religion to come to a clairvoyant grasp of what religion itself is. Philosophy helps religion to rise from unanalyzed faith to reason; that is, since philosophy and religion have the same material object, namely, objective eternal truth, or the absolute God, philosophy, by substituting conscious rational knowledge for the obscure intent of faith, helps religion to understand what it was doing and so to understand itself. Another way of saying the same thing is that philosophy places the religious striving of man in a context, that, namely, of mature human self-understanding: philosophy sees "philosophy of religion," or religion that understands itself rationally, as a part of the whole that is philosophy.[91]

The full richness of this point of view, however, becomes evident only when one is careful to keep in mind what philosophy itself is. It is for Hegel—to some extent, it might be added, just as it was for Aquinas[92]—a participation in the divine mind. If through mature self-understanding religion sees that it is, materially, an integral part of the philosophic enterprise, by the same understanding philosophy sees that it is a participation, indeed, a necessary mediating element, in the very life of the absolute. The true philosopher is one spirit with God. If, then, for Schleiermacher religion is simply a matter of feeling, for Hegel it is the consciousness of the unity of the divine and the human. Indeed, it is

> the self-consciousness of God, or the absolute spirit; or the idea of spirit that relates itself to itself; the relationship of the spirit to the absolute spirit; the self-knowledge of the divine spirit. This self-knowledge of spirit, however, is mediated through the finite spirit, that is, through the consciousness that as such the finite consciousness is. Religion thus has the finite consciousness within it, but as a finite that is cancelled and transcended; for the "other" whereof the absolute spirit knows is it itself, and so it is the absolute spirit, primarily, that knows itself.[93]

One might say, Baur continues, that human religion is how, concretely, or in the dispensation that in fact obtains, God knows himself. The content of religion is the self-consciousness of God: God-in-man knowing God. "God, therefore, is, in a word, this: to distinguish self from self, to be an object for self, but in this distinction to be simply identical with self."[94]

It might be added that if the orthodox-minded reader is tempted to wonder why God has to go to all this trouble to know himself, the answer lies in the sharp rejection of anthropomorphism characteristic of German religious thinking of the romantic and early post-romantic periods. How—or if—God knows him-

---

[91] *Ibid.*, p. 669.

[92] An extremely interesting and highly detailed carrying out of this parallel is to be found in Albert Chapelle, *Hegel et la religion* (Paris, 1964ff.). Two volumes (with a collection of ancillary texts) of Chapelle's projected three-volume study have already appeared. have already appeared.

[93] *Ibid.*, pp. 672f.

[94] *Gnosis*, p. 675.

self, so to speak, "all by himself," is hidden from us: it is evident, however, that
he knows himself through us, who live, inescapably, *chez Dieu.* Thus we are free
to speak of this second kind of knowledge as, philosophico-religiously, a "sure
thing." From the Hegelian point of view, to grasp that God and we truly are by
the power of the same truth is not at all problematic; it is simply human
maturity. The feeling or consciousness of this unity of the human and the divine,
Baur continues, is love, "and God is love, that is, this distinction and the
nothingness of this distinction, that play of distinction in which there is no real
earnest, that play of love with itself wherein being-another, or separation, or
division, is not taken seriously, the positing of distinction precisely as cancelled,
the simple eternal idea."[95] The vocation of man is to understand that this great
game is going on, to participate in it consciously.

Hegelianism, for all that, is not euphoria. The foregoing observations refer
to what man ought to be, to how his basic ontological status ought to expand
into consciousness; they do not necessarily describe man as he happens to exist,
that is, as he perhaps somewhat superficially understands himself—or, as Hegel
would say, as he is for himself. The state of consciousness in which man thinks
of himself primarily as "another mind" in distinction from the divine is a
betrayal of the radical truth of humanity: in a word, it is evil. As Baur puts it,
"Because man is spirit, he is, if he lives only according to nature, evil; his natural
being is Evil."[96] On the other hand, man does not achieve redemption and peace
through violence: if nature is what keeps him from God and self-understanding,
it is also only through nature—since nature is how, in fact, man is—that redemption from evil can come to man. As a result, says Baur, "Here is . . . the place
where, in the Hegelian philosophy of religion, we see that the history of religion
is to be inserted as an integral part into the structure of the system."[97]

Natural man works out his salvation in fear, trembling, and history, for so is
natural man constituted. Through the various moments of the historical religions, the successive moments of the faltering manifestation in man of the
concept of religion, man's goal is to arrive at that final stage wherein "the
religious consciousness is not distinguished from the concept, the idea, the
perfectly realized concept, absolute religion." What will happen then is that "the
finite . . . is through the work of the spirit put aside, it is nothingness, and this
nothingness has become evident to the consciousness of the spirit, the free and
therefore infinite spirit."[98] In and through history man, or better, the divine
spirit in man frees man from sin and finitude, frees him, for that matter from
history. Definitive humanity, duly expanded human consciousness, definitive
human freedom or selfhood comes precisely in the realization, in the grasping by

[95] *Ibid.,* p. 677.
[96] *Ibid.,* p. 687.
[97] *Ibid.,* p. 689.
[98] *Ibid.,* p. 690.

the human spirit, of its idea, namely, that it is really one spirit with the at once necessary and free absolute God. Such a state of affairs is well termed absolute religion.

The emergence of absolute religion is the incarnation. It could not be otherwise, for

> if what the nature of spirit, the nature of God, or God as spirit is is to be revealed to man, so must God as spirit appear in the form of immediacy, in sensuous presence, . . . for that only is certain for man which, in an immediate manner, is before his inner and outer vision.[99]

It must be stressed, however, that this certitude arises only from a *combination* of inner and outer vision; that is to say, man does not attain to absolute religion by assenting to the external facts of the life of God incarnate. That would be a contradiction in terms. What happens is rather that man's inner, or spiritual, vision penetrates to the inner, spiritual meaning of the reports about the Christ. After the death of Christ the spirit comes upon his followers; the followers' spiritual insight, or faith, *is* God as spirit, and conversely, "this spirit as existing is the community."[100] Baur continues:

> Faith is not about the external temporal history that lies before it in sensuous fashion; rather is the sensuous content transformed into an entirely different, spiritual, divine content. This latter is posited as self-conscious knowledge of him [Christ] in the element of consciousness, of inwardness. . . . The sensuous history is only the point of departure for faith; its point of arrival is the turning back of spirit into itself, spiritual consciousness. . . . The true Christian faith-content is to be established by philosophy, not by faith. What the spirit does is not history. It concerns itself only with that which is present.[101]

When the finite spirit becomes present to its true—infinite—self through faith, it sees that its finitude and sin are in fact entitively nothing. More precisely, "Faith is itself the divine spirit that works in the subject, in the spirit of the subject. In faith is the naturalness of the subject worked against, finished off, removed."[102] By baptism is signified man's inclusion in the ambit of this divine action, and by the eucharist its continuing efficacy is sensuously made present to him. He need not fear: he is redeemed, for God is being reconciled with God in and through him. He is free to realize the effect of the divine power in his daily life, for "the true atonement, through which the divine realizes itself in the field of actuality, consists in moral and lawful civic life . . . ."[103]

[99]*Ibid.,* pp. 692f.

[100]*Ibid.,* p. 696.

[101]*Ibid.*

[102]*Ibid.,* p. 697.

[103]*Ibid.,* p. 699.

Baur now takes up two obvious objections, the first being that the God of Hegel does not look very much like the God of Abraham, Isaac, and Jacob. He is not personal, not, above all, free to create or not to create the universe.[104] Baur replies that this denigration of both God and Hegel arises from a double misunderstanding of anthropomorphism. God must not be spoken of as if God were man writ large: that man has the immediate, superficial, perhaps, experience of freedom of choice in no way contradicts the solid ontological principle that the absolute, as such, is the synthesis or ground of freedom and necessity. On the other hand, if God cannot be conceived of at all apart from our conception of the universe, it is nonetheless true that the presence of the world does not make God cease to be God. After all, even the best that we have to work with in speaking of God is merely our conception of the *identity* of the divine *and the human* as presented in absolute religion. If we are scandalized at the built-in anthropomorphism of objective religion—ultimately the at least incipient understanding of the identity of the divine and the human—all we can do is either to cease to be religious or to lapse into romantic subjectivism. In the end, the two are pretty much the same thing.

The second objection to which Baur addresses himself is that Hegelianism seems to dispense with the historical Christ.[105] Here Baur goes back over the ground that Schleiermacher trod so uncertainly. Baur replies by making what he has already said of the Christ of history somewhat more precise. There are three ways in which one may look upon the Christ, those, namely, of history, of faith, and of philosophy. These three kinds or levels of knowing are intimately, indeed, causally, related: still, they must be carefully distinguished. Without the Christ of history, the Christ who was sensuously perceptible to his contemporaries and about whom certain facts can be established by purely historical research, there could not have been a Christ of faith. (True, the whole religious history of the west might have been different, but it profits nothing, really, to indulge in such speculation; what has actually taken place is that western religiosity has in large part arisen from the life, death, and teaching of Jesus Christ—as historical research is quite able to show.)[106] On the other hand, the Christ of history, even if a necessary condition for the emergence of the Christ of faith, is by no means to be identified with the Christ of faith. Faith, the second level of knowing mentioned above, looks upon Christ as the God-man; it is one thing to say that Christian faith would not have arisen without the Christ of history and quite another to say that the object of faith is the Christ of history, for historical

---

[104]*Ibid.*, pp. 700-706.

[105]*Ibid.*, pp. 707-21.

[106]It is probably correct to say, as Hodgson does, *Formation,* pp. 64 and 73, that Baur was much more interested in historical-critical studies than Hegel, who, for all that he had to say about history, apparently did not think that critical historical work might force him to modify his metaphysical-historical principles. See Frederick Copleston, *A History of Philosophy,* VII (Garden City, New York, 1965), Part I, 261-69.

study is quite incapable of verifying God-manhood. Christ, Baur says, is "all that he is as God-man only in faith and through faith. The God-man is indeed the object of faith, but not the necessary presupposition of faith; what faith has for its presupposition is Christ not as God-man but as simple man, as human appearance."[107] Faith, it might be said, is an affirmation of the truth of the God-man, which affirmation results from the action of the divine spiritualizing force in and through the community. Even if this act of faith is caused—in the sense of historically occasioned—by the historical Christ, properly speaking it is caused by and proceeds from the lively inwardness of the believer-in-community (bearing in mind that the community is spirit-as-existing). In no sense is faith, as such, grounded upon empirical evidence, even when it determines to *believe* that certain elements of the history of the Christ were "historical events." The appearance of the historical Christ simply evokes in the community certain energies which had hitherto lain dormant.

Spirit active in man, however, does not stop at the level of faith but moves on, in an analogous manner, to the third level, that of philosophy. The believer begins to understand himself and that in which he has believed—indeed he understands that he and the object of his belief are in fact one: the man of faith, in truth, is one spirit with God and his Christ.

> The knowledge of Christ as the God-man is, in this respect, nothing other than . . . the knowledge of the truth that man has a true existence only in his generality, that spirit does not have a true existence as finite spirit—or the consciousness of the unity of divine and human nature. Thus what in the first moment is a human appearance is in the second a divine appearance; in the third it is the pure idea, spirit in itself. All that rests on the life and appearance of Christ has its truth only in the fact that in him the essence and life of spirit presents itself.[108]

The dogma of the incarnation is now understood, not as historical fact (such as faith, albeit in a non-historical mode, was wont to grasp it), but as "an eternal determination of the essence of God, by reason of which God becomes man in time (in each individual man) only insofar as he is man from eternity."[109] The dogmas about the death, resurrection, and ascension of Christ are now understood as figurative presentations of the loving self-comprehension of God (in whom, so to speak, man is "included"). The symbol of Christ-as-God-man is now to be understood as "man in his universality, not a single individual, but the universal individual."[110] To sum up, it may be said that even though the Christ of history, so far as we know, was apparently unable to express himself with the philosophical cogency of later ages, he it was who first became clearly conscious

[107]*Gnosis,* p. 713.

[108]*Ibid.,* p. 715.

[109]*Ibid.*

[110]*Ibid.*

of what it means to be the Christ, *clearly conscious of what we all are.* At the level of philosophy we understand that *Christhood* is maturely self-conscious *manhood.*

Everything hinges, Baur insists, on whether the distinction between faith and philosophical reason is an absolute or a relative distinction.[111] Naturally, if faith and reason are absolutely to be distinguished, that is, if they are in no way points along a continuum of levels in an ascending process, faith must be conceded to be the highest truth. The dogmas of faith, after all, are what reason in the sense of philosophy of religion is "about." On the other hand, if faith and reason are but relatively distinct, if, to put it another way, they differ as to form but not as to fundamental content, then reason must be followed to the uttermost limit. Philosophy, now, could be deprived of this primacy only if it could be proved that it cancels out, not only the form, but also the very content of faith—and who could ever prove that? "How, though, is such a demonstration to be conducted, since the system emphatically asserts just what constitutes the content of the doctrine of Christ as God-man, the unity of divine and human nature?"[112]

Baur's explicit conclusion is that the ideal Christ of Hegel is quite different from the ideal Christ of Schleiermacher. The difference is that for Hegel the ideal Christ is not merely postulated but rather seen in and through the historical Christ. In fact, only in Hegel's thought is the historicity of the ideal Christ (that is, the underlying unity of the two "poles" of Christhood) recognized in its full scope. If the God-man is the oneness of the divine and the human, so is the *historical Christ,* strictly speaking, all those who realize absolute religion by understanding themselves as members of his body. In humanity thus striving for conscious unity with its divine essence in Christ's community that is

> ever growing, ever taking into itself the fullness of the spirit, the God-man Christ, who is ever present in the truth and actuality of history, celebrates the victory of life over death, the eternal feast of his resurrection and ascension. Thus this philosophy of religion is by no means lacking in a very concrete concept of the historical Christ.[113]

[111]*Ibid.,* pp. 717-20.

[112]*Ibid.,* p. 719.

[113]*Ibid.,* p. 721. See above, p. 10, n. 20. With regard to *when* Baur familiarized himself with the thought of Hegel, Hodgson, *op. cit.,* pp. 23f., points out that "Baur specifically stated that Hegel's philosophy was brought under consideration and influenced his own work for the first time in *Die christliche Gnosis.* This evidence would seem to indicate the winter of 1834-35 (and perhaps the preceding months as well) as the period in which Baur first studied Hegel's philosophy." Baur's statement appears in one of the chapters he contributed to K. Klüpfel, ed., *Geschichte und Beschreibung der Universität Tübingen* (Tübingen, 1849), "Die evangelisch-theologische Fakultät vom Jahr 1812," p. 407. Baur certainly, in view of his troubles over Strauss, did not want to appear, in 1849, as an apostle of Hegelianism; moreover, he is simply telling the truth when he says that prior to 1835 Hegel, *nominatim,* did not play any particular role in his published works. But this

Baur ends *Die christliche Gnosis* with the observation that there is really no half-way house between making an absolute of mythic faith and openly admitting that philosophy of religion, or gnosis, is the crown of human religiosity.[114] If philosophy of religion, far from destroying the data with which it works, renders these data truly intelligible in the manner that has been sketched here, it amply

fact says nothing about the degree of Baur's actual acquaintance with Hegel's writings. That, as Zeller states, *op. cit.,* p. 401, Baur first publicly, if obliquely, embraced Hegelianism in the *Gegensatz* seems beyond question, a point which Hodgson partially concedes in *Ferdinand Christian Baur,* p. 4, and which can be inferred from the passages quoted in Chapter III of this study.

Quite another question is that of *the extent to which* Baur was a Hegelian. I am inclined to answer, "Quite fully, except in matters of detail." After all, the *only* adverse criticism of Hegel in *Gnosis* bears on his discussion of heathenism and Judaism (pp. 721-35), *not* on his discussion of Christianity. Hodgson, *Formation,* p. 62, n. 91, gives a brief summary of an exchange between Zeller and Albrecht Ritschl over whether Baur, in pp. 712ff. of *Gnosis,* was merely reporting on Hegel or actually agreeing with him regarding the historical Christ. Hodgson and Zeller opt for the first interpretation: paraphrase only; Ritschl, for the second: agreement, but with the observation that Hegel and Baur too sharply separate the historical and the ideal Christ. I am tempted to find in this dispute a re-enactment of the fabled blind man and the elephant. It is hard to see how any statement of Baur's on p. 717 of the *Gnosis* is (as claimed by Zeller and Hodgson) an indictment of Hegel. The closest thing is the question, "How could faith in him [Christ] as the God-man have arisen unless he were in some manner objective, such as faith takes him to be?" Well, Baur's answer to his self-posed rhetorical question is clear enough: "The necessary presupposition is in any case that truth in itself, the unity of the divine and human nature, came first in Christ to concrete truth, to self-conscious knowledge, and was as truth uttered and taught by him." The elephant that seems to have eluded observation is precisely Hegel's–and Baur's–massive insistence on the *participation* of the historical in the supra-historical: to repeat, Christ comprehended *first*–so far as we know–what we all are, that is, that we and Christ, as historical beings, participate equally in the same divine ground of the historical. All that Hegelianism seems to be saying on this point is that *somebody,* sooner or later, would break through to a fuller understanding of the real dignity of man. To insist that sooner or later *somebody* would have invented the telephone does not lessen the historical objectivity of Alexander Graham Bell; he found what was there to be found, true, but he really found it. It is all very well if one is not satisfied with the insufficiently orthodox character of Hegelian Christology, with the idea that Jesus Christ discovered what *simpliciter* all men, himself included, all are; it seems excessive, however, to assert that for Hegelianism there could have arisen a Christianity without there having been a historical Christ. Such an assertion is all but a contradiction in terms.

Perhaps Baur himself ought to have the last word. In 1836, in his less than successful attempt to dissociate himself from Strauss's version of Hegelianism he wrote: "I am a disciple of no philosophical system, for I well know how deceptive it is to make oneself dependent upon human authority; at the same time, though, I am convinced that theology can learn much from Hegel. I also think that many of those who are so ready to express an opinion on him would judge otherwise if they could make up their minds first to become better acquainted with his writings." "Abgenöthigte Erklärung gegen einen Artikel der evangelischen Kirchenzeitung, herausgegeben von D. E. W. Hengstenberg, Prof. der Theol. an der Universität zu Berlin, Mai 1836," reprinted in *Ausgewählte Werke,* ed. Klaus Scholder, I (Stuttgart-Bad Cannstatt: Frommann, 1963f.), 313ff.

[114]*Gnosis,* pp. 735-40.

justifies itself, One must only bear in mind that, whatever one may think of the most recent actual attempts at religious philosophy, such philosophizing can never be thought of as completed, for it is the ongoing work of the spirit in man. It is progressive, however, in the sense of *cumulative*. Baur emphasizes that "just as, from the beginning on, Christian philosophy of religion could develop only on the foundation of objective Christianity, so the same foundation [is one] from which it can never sever itself."[115] If, then, gnosis is justifiable in principle, so is writing the history of gnosis from the beginnings to Hegel.

In Baur's *Gegensatz* and "Erwiederung" certain views on both divine and human freedom, and on the personality and work of Christ were put forth as the proper nineteenth-century flowering of sixteenth-century Protestantism. As his justification for so advancing such views Baur insisted on the developmental character of maturely self-conscious, that is, Protestant, Christianity. As opposed to Catholicism, Protestantism knows how to distinguish between religious form and content in such a way as to retain both in the most fitting manner—the content as ever more surely possessed, the form as, not the single event, but the "manifestational" process in which this possession continuously occurs. In the careful appropriation of Hegel's philosophy of religion that we find exemplified in Baur's *Die christliche Gnosis* we are given a quite formal statement of the theological options adumbrated in Baur's controversial works. For the Baur of 1834-36, at least, the link between the sixteenth and the nineteenth centuries was forged with Hegelian alloy.

Afterwards

The Roman professor Bellarmine could safely take on the whole Protestant world. Bishop Bossuet could safely count on the favor of Louis XIV. Möhler, unfortunately, was protected neither by geography nor patronage. In a town as small as Tübingen in a principality as small as Württemberg, in a *Protestant* town as small as Tübingen, the Möhler-Baur controversy was one of those squabbles that simply *had* to be ended. And one is hardly surprised over how it did in fact end. Möhler had to go.

We are told that Möhler's students saw him to the coach with a torchlight procession, and withal, much grief. About more substantive points regarding his departure from Tübingen there is rather less information available. All that can be said with assurance is that after life in Tübingen had been made rather unpleasant for Möhler, he was allowed to resign and to accept a place that had been offered him at the newly reconstituted University in Munich. He began to teach there in spring, 1835.[116]

There is no evidence to suggest that Baur was directly responsible for Möhler's giving up his post as Tübingen. Such descriptions of Baur's character as

[115]*Ibid.*, p. 740.

[116]For biographical source-material, see above, p.   , n. 22.

have been left by his intimates and students lead one to doubt that he would have stooped to low tactics to rid himself—and Protestantism—of an embarrassment. It is true, of course, that Baur criticized Möhler as a disturber of the peace, but given the long-standing religious antagonisms of provincial Germany—as well as the too brief respite of the Enlightenment—this was not an unreasonable point for Baur to make. Moreover, Baur was actually told to his face by King Wilhelm that *he* was a disturber of the peace![117]

At any rate, quite apart from the situation at Tübingen, the subsequently celebrated Ignaz Döllinger of the Munich faculty had been for some time attempting to secure Möhler's services for the Bavarian capital. In a letter from Möhler to Döllinger dated February 26, 1835, the former confirms a previously expressed willingness to accept the chair of church history at Munich. "Rather some good Catholic Bavarian beer than the oldest Prussian Rhine wine—and the same goes for its neighbor Neckar wine!"[118] In the same letter Möhler notes that from the king and his advisors he is expecting a censorship ruling: no more writing on touchy subjects. Surely to a theological man of letters and church historian like Möhler censorship would have been unbearable, but had he already suffered other, if pettier, annoyances? We do not know. He does remark, however, in a letter to Adam Gengler, dated September 19, 1834, that "you can live much more quietly in Bamberg and in a whole year not experience anything like how unbearable these people are. Every Protestant thinks he is a born sage."[119] It is hard to say whether Möhler was thinking merely that there were more Protestants in Tübingen (which was the case, it would seem), or that the Protestants in Tübingen were more unpleasant than usual.

Again, exactly what the king's advisors would have done had Möhler not requested to be released from his post remains unknown. Nonetheless, in a covering letter for Möhler's request, the *Kultusminister,* von Schlayer, makes the following moderate, even sympathetic observations:

> The distinguished scientific formation and activity of this . . . man is known everywhere, and his departure from the *Landesuniversität* is beyond question to be considered a loss to it and to the Catholic faculty. . . . It would seem that this zealous man, who in his opinions stands closer to the papal system than many other distinguished theologians, could hope sooner to satisfy his desires in a predominantly Catholic state, one with an ampler hierarchical development than could come about in the situation here.[120]

---

[117]Thus, in effect, Baur to his friend L. F. Heyd; see Hodgson, *Formation,* pp. 18f., nn. 74-75. The remark was made in 1841, after Baur had engaged in several additional disputes.

[118]The letter is given in full in Lösch-Möhler, *Aktenstücke u. Briefe,* pp. 241-42. Attempts had also been made to obtain Möhler's services for the University of Bonn (which was under Prussian rule).

[119]Lösch, *Gengler,* p. 125.

The king granted Möhler's request, without comment, on April 8, 1835.

Finally, there is no evidence that either Möhler or Baur planned to continue the controversy. Baur was already deeply involved in the uproar surrounding the *Leben Jesu* of his sometime student D. F. Strauss, and his failure to convince his contemporaries that his kind of Hegelianism was substantially different from that of Strauss seriously damaged his reputation. The cloud was not to lift until a good many years after his death in 1860. Möhler's health had begun gravely to deteriorate as early as 1828, and the combined strain of the controversy and of moving to new surroundings proved too much for him. He died on April 12, 1838, at the age of forty-two.

Möhler's accomplishment was aptly enough for the times summed up in these lines spoken some seven years after his death:

> This flourishing of Catholicism, this strengthening of its consciousness, belongs to the most recent period, in which oppositions of principle have tended to be sharpened as much as possible. Among the manifestations in which the consciousness of the times . . . most clearly embodies itself, one of the first places goes to Möhler's *Symbolik*.[121]

The speaker was F. C. Baur.

[120] Lösch-Möhler, *Aktenstücke u. Briefe,* pp. 412-13. In plainer terms, von Schlayer was relieved that the scholar who was rather too much a Catholic-hierarchical "organization man" was going somewhere else!

[121] F. C. Baur, *Kirchengeschichte des Neunzehnten Jahrhunderts,* ed. E. Zeller (Tübingen, 1862), p. 309. In another letter to his frequent correspondent Gengler, dated December 12, 1834 (Losch, *Gengler,* pp. 134-35), Mohler evinces a similar conception of his role: "Catholics lack courage, self-respect, full, conscious trust in the inner worth of the causes to which they devote themselves. The awakening of these I hold to be a great and holy task, and . . . I do all that I can, so as at least partially to accomplish it. . . . Without faith, courage, self-respect and trust all bound together there can never be any science in *Catholic* circles."

CHAPTER V

Epilogue

Möhler's critique of Protestantism and Baur's defense of it are in many ways surprising to the twentieth-century reader. In the first place, such a reader wonders at almost every point how faithfully these two men carry out what has been called the first task of historical theology, the presentation of the content of documents from the past. Quite simply, is either of them well enough acquainted with Reformation-period Protestantism to make a credible assessment of it?[1] It would be impractical in a study such as the present one to examine Möhler's and Baur's knowledge of the various confessions at literally every point. But neither is such an examination called for. Since the Möhler-Baur controversy centered on the meaning of Protestantism, and since both Möhler and Baur tended to deduce the characteristic doctrines of Protestantism from the Protestant positions on original justice and original sin, it should suffice here to examine what the primary documents most relevant to the controversy have to say on these points. The materials in question are Article II, "Original Sin," and Article XVIII, "Free Will," of the Apology of the Augsburg Confession; and Article I "Original Sin," and Article II, "Free Will," of Part II of the Formula of Concord.[2]

In the Apology Melanchthon points out that in the Augsburg Confession itself "we wanted simply to describe what original sin includes."[3] Briefly, Lutheran[4] teaching means "that in those who are born according to the flesh we deny the existence not only of actual fear and trust in God but also of the possibility and gifts to produce it."[5] To describe the effect of original sin in such a way as to leave human nature the same after as before is, on the contrary, to deny that original sin had any effect at all: "To be able to love God above all things by one's own power and to obey his commandments, what else is this but to have original righteousness? If human nature has such powers that by itself it can love God above all things, as the scholastics confidently assert, then what can original sin be?"[6] The point is simply that human nature, as it exists after

---

[1] Möhler's and Baur's assessments of classical Catholic orthodoxy will not be reconsidered here because (a) Möhler is generally regarded today as an orthodox and well-informed Catholic theologian; and (b) Baur's occasional lapses have been corrected by Möhler himself.

[2] See *BK*, 57, 311-13, 843-912.

[3] *Apology*, II, 1, Eng., p. 100.

[4] Inasmuch as Möhler and Baur move with ease from the generalization *Protestantism* to *Lutheranism*, etc., the same practice will be followed here—though not without scruple.

[5] *Ibid.*, II, 2, p. 100.

the fall, either has or has not the power to love God above all things. The Catholic scholastics say that it has; the Lutherans, that it has not. Now, the root of what must be accounted the scholastics' error is that they

> mingled Christian doctrine with philosophical views about the perfection of nature and attributed more than was proper to free will and to "elicited acts." They taught that men are justified before God by philosophical or civic righteousness, which we agree is subject to reason and somewhat in our power. But thereby they failed to see the inner uncleanness of human nature. This cannot be adjudged except from the Word of God, which the scholastics do not often employ in their discussions.[7]

What must be emphasized, on the one hand, is that it is in principle impossible for philosophy alone ever to know that such virtuous acts as reason may elicit from man's faculties are not radically virtuous. More precisely, the good man of philosophy acts out of self-will, out of the desire and will to be virtuous; philosophy cannot know that even such virtue as this does not suffice to make a man just before God. It merely *looks* virtuous; *unknown* to philosophy *as such,* a vitiating inner uncleanness (that is, precisely self-will) remains in man. On the other hand, to say that such acts as a philosopher, in the absence of evidence to the contrary, would term good are not such as will justify a man before God is by no means to say that man has no capacity at all for virtue or lacks its basic faculty, free will. Melanchthon explains:

> We are not denying freedom to the human will. The human will has freedom to choose among the works and things which reason by itself can grasp. To some extent it can achieve civil righteousness or the righteousness of works. It can [for example] talk about God and express its worship of him in outward works. . . . [But] it is false to say that a man does not sin if, outside the state of grace, he does the works prescribed in the commandments. . . . Without the Holy Spirit human hearts . . . are ungodly.[8]

In sum, it may fairly be said that according to the Apology human nature is altered for the worse in original sin, but it is not so altered as to be deprived of rational freedom, even though the exercise of such freedom cannot make man *fundamentally* just before God.

In the Formula of Concord certain precisions are added to these views. First, with respect to the term *nature* the framers of this document note that "if one wishes to speak strictly, one must maintain a distinction between (a) our nature as it is created and preserved by God and in which sin dwells and

---

[6]*Ibid.,* II, 9f., p. 102. About whom, precisely is Melanchthon speaking? Biel, perhaps? Melanchthon's reasoning appears to be elliptical: a possible elaboration would be that if God promises to give grace to any man who does what he can to merit it (*de congruo*), that man, "by himself," brings it about that he is enabled to "love God above all things."

[7]*Ibid.,* II, 12f., p. 102.

[8]*Ibid.,* XVIII, 4ff., p. 225.

(b) original sin itself which dwells in the nature."[9] A distinction may also be made between this strict sense of *nature* and the loose, conversational sense in which, if it is said, for example, "'It is the serpent's nature to bite and poison,' the term *nature* means . . . a disposition or characteristic. It is in this latter sense that Luther writes that sin and sinning are men's disposition and nature."[10] The point here is that it is not man's nature as such that is evil, but rather that a man is evil because he is "accidentally"[11] afflicted with sin. It is stressed, in addition, that not every instance of an expression common to daily speech *and* to philosophy or theology should be understood in terms of the *latter* possibility.

Secondly, with respect to the role which man's free will plays in justification, "although man's reason or natural intellect still has a dim spark of the knowledge that there is a God, as well as the teaching of the law," it is nevertheless the case that

> prior to his conversion not a spark of spiritual power has remained or exists in man by which he could make himself ready for the grace of God or to accept the proferred grace, nor that he has any capacity for grace by and for himself or can apply himself to it or prepare himself for it, or help, do, effect, or cooperate toward his conversion by his own powers, either altogether or halfway or in the tiniest or smallest degree.[12]

The "synergism" of the Catholics and their sympathizers is thus ruled out, and the principle that human nature and operation in the present state of man's existence are incommensurate with man's need for justification is carried out with entire consistency. It is not simply that, unaided, man cannot in some observable fashion *do* anything toward his justification; man cannot even hold himself in a state of receptivity adequate simply to *receiving* justification, in the sense of permitting God to act upon him. In the sections of the Apology and the Formula of Concord under discussion a single theme is constantly reiterated: according to the most certain and most complete information we have about man's nature, this nature, whatever else it once could or now can do, is unable, *now,* to cleanse itself, not of "sins" in a superficial sense, but of sin in the sense of an absolutely primary disorientation from God. One is not meant to trace the continuity of nature between man's state before the fall and after it: rather is discontinuity to be emphasized. *Nature,* when it is being used as a technical term, refers to what *in fact* man is or was in one or other condition: it is not to be taken as denoting a philosophical possibility that could be indifferently actualized in either state. In other words, the rule according to which man's nature is discussed here is not philosophy but the word of God.

[9]*Ibid., Formula,* I, 33, p. 514.
[10]*Ibid.,* 51, p. 517.
[11]*Ibid.,* 61, p. 519.
[12]*Ibid.,* II, 7, p. 521.

It is only too clear that Baur's objection to Möhler's use of these texts is wholly valid.[13] Möhler *does* quote them out of context, because he consistently ignores the distinction made between a philosophical and a theological point of view. He wilfully treats texts describing man's innermost standing before God independently of the context in which they were made and implicitly, therefore, as philosophical delineations of human nature. Nonetheless, Möhler's objection to Baur's use of these texts is *also* wholly valid! The lack of proportion between human nature and justification is treated here as absolute and constant, but Baur treats it as merely relative to a certain inchoate state of nature, as tending to disappear. If Möhler extends the foregoing description of original sin beyond its proper context, Baur largely fails to take it seriously even in the context in which it was given. One is thus forced to conclude that in the central point of their systematic presentation of the Reformers' doctrine both Möhler and Baur failed grievously as symbolical-historical theologians. Each, rather perplexingly, saw the mote in his brother's eye but not the beam in his own.

Be that as it may, such a judgment as has just been made is somewhat too severe. All that has really been said is that Möhler and Baur did not write intellectual history in the manner of reputable twentieth-century historical theologians. No matter what one may think of their representation of classical Protestantism, however, one must also grant that, by and large, they were conscious of the disparities between their presentations and the primary documents. Möhler, after all, explicitly undertook to explain the Reformers' positions better than they themselves had done. Baur, for his part, constantly stressed the developmental character of Protestantism, calling attention to the fact that his manner of speaking was very different from the Reformers' more homiletic style. What is it, then, that Möhler and Baur were trying to do?

If one imagines a kind of scale with mere historical reporting at one extreme and historical interpretation at the other, the work of these two men will clearly be located many degrees closer to "interpretation" than to "reporting." Basically what they did was to make highly self-conscious interpretations of Reformation-period documents—without stating sufficiently to please the twentieth-century reader what might be the preliminaries to such interpretations. Even, then, if they did not clearly establish the facts to be interpreted and the mental steps involved in generating the interpretations, what they were

---

[13]Both Vermeil, *op. cit.,* pp. 233-68, and Vigener, *op. cit.,* pp. 37-75, support the argument advanced here, viz., that Möhler seriously misunderstood the intent of the Protestant confessions; despite their valuable analysis of Möhler's procedure, however, both Vermeil and Vigener fail to give due weight to the positive side of Möhler's work. By not attending sufficiently to his over-arching conception of ecclesiastical tradition they thus fail to appreciate the full logic of his approach. Regarding Baur, both Zeller, *Vorträge u. Abhandlungen,* pp. 437-41, and Pfleiderer, *op. cit.,* p. 285, agree that Baur would have done better to separate nineteenth-century concerns from sixteenth-century history. They are, again, entirely correct—but such a separation was just what Baur, by his "gnosis," was trying to avoid!

fundamentally about is clear enough. Möhler meant to compare the various confessions with the truths of Christian reason and the gospel. Baur asked it to be assumed that the various confessions are all manifestations of the absolute and of man's relationship to the absolute, it being understood that it is in principle possible to see that certain of these manifestations are purer or more highly developed than others. In fairness to Möhler and Baur, therefore, further questions should be raised. It is my contention that even if things go awry in Möhler's and Baur's reporting, their handling of the interpretative side of historical theology sheds more than a little light on the structure and possibilities of this discipline. Möhler's basic interpretative tool is the concept of the living tradition of Catholicism.[14] Baur's is what he terms Christian gnosis, or religion become philosophically conscious of itself. What, as regards the second task of historical theology, can be said of the merits of each?

The comparison of living tradition and Christian gnosis as interpretative tools is by no means an easy task. It might seem at first that such a comparison is simply the evaluation of a higher order of opposed claims. Instead, for example, of trying to determine whether the authority of the pope or that of scripture should claim the primary allegiance of the believer, is it not simply that a presumably more systematically-minded believer is asked to choose between tradition and "gnosis"? The answer is No, for the reason that an adherent of gnosis is not simply a believer. The reason, again, is that (a) an adherent of gnosis claims to be quite as orthodox as any believer, only more consciously so, and (b) an adherent of tradition claims that a substantial part of what he believes is in principle verifiable by reason active in historical research. In a word, neither the traditionist nor the gnostic is exclusively a believer or a rationalist. In the schematism of opposed claims, which is inappropriate to the Möhler-Baur controversy, the claims in question are addressed to believers who, under the guidance of the Spirit, are to opt for one of them, or who, as rational human beings, can decide which set of *prolegomena fidei* is the more persuasive. The spheres of *dogmata* and *prolegomena* are kept wholly separate. In a comparison of tradition and gnosis, on the other hand, the terms of comparison are two states or modes of the *interpenetration* of faith and reason. Herein lies the unique interest of the Möhler-Baur controversy. Interpenetration, of course,

---

[14]There is considerable justification for suggesting, as a kind of handy overview, that Möhler was a kind of Catholic Kierkegaard. Möhler, of course, emphasizes characteristic Catholic doctrines, but Kierkegaard occasionally did the same; even the most striking difference between the two men's religious outlook, that of the relationship between individual and community, is, for Kierkegaard, open to dispute. It is surprising that this rather obvious parallel has not received greater currency. A much more frequent parallel, that between Möhler and Newman, has received much greater, and usually mistaken, notice; the case is well discussed in H. Tristram, "J. A. Möhler et J. N. Newman: la pensée allemande et la renaissance catholique en Angleterre," *Revue des sciences philosophiques et théologiques,* XXVII (1938), 184-204. Tristram concludes that it is improbable that Möhler had any appreciable influence on Newman.

does not mean confusion. Just as such a confrontation does not call for a blank either-or between faith and reason, so does it not call for a blurring of the boundary between faith and reason, particularly if *reason* be expanded to include poetic insight. The question is how a Christian who is both a believer and, precisely as a Christian, a rational, history-conscious man can hold belief and history-conscious reason together.

The problem that Schleiermacher's theology raised for Baur as well as for his Catholic colleagues at Tübingen was that of how the self-consciousness of the religious individual is to come into contact with the historical Christ and his church—which problem, to be sure, is simply the religious dimension of the polarizing of individual and collectivity that began to be acute in the decades after Napoleon and has continued to be so ever since. As a resolution of this problem, the traditionist approach of Möhler and thinkers like him has the great advantage of taking the manifestation of God in history with the utmost serious-ness. What is perhaps an equally great disadvantage is that it does so, at least to an unsympathetic observer, in a highly erratic fashion. It is, it claims, based on the direct inspiration of the Spirit. That there is a living tradition of creed and cult proceeding from the historical Jesus onward is something that is believed in a free surrender to the guiding impulse of the Spirit. Belief and positive doubt are contraries: for those to whom this approach is satisfying it is satisfying because it is absolutely certain, absolutely trustworthy as the basis for passionate religiosity. The difficulty is that believers of this kind are incapable of giving a fully rational account of why they hold what they do. They are led by the Spirit: those who do not comprehend can only be invited to pray that they, too, might become men whose lives are hidden in God. In fairness to the traditionist it must be borne in mind that his apparent arrogance is in fact the direct result of his worshipful sense of the transcendence of God.

It is clear that the traditionist's belief in the objective continuity of incarna-tion, sacraments, and church effectively keeps him from falling into the trap of Schleiermacher's disjunction of the ideal and the historical. Or so it seems. The difficulty is that there is still a complete discontinuity between the kinds of assertions that the traditionist wants to make about "what really happened." What he ultimately holds as to the nature and significance of what happened, he holds through belief, not historical research. He already believes what historical research, properly carried out, must, in part at least, discover for itself. Hence, if historical redemption is taken entirely seriously, the historical study of historical redemption is not. In practice it is left to apologetics, a part of the study of the *prolegomena fidei,* and is never really formally integrated into the study of dogmatics. Needless to say, in a weak spirit such a state of mind is inimical to care in historical research, even in apologetics! For a strong spirit, nevertheless, historical research becomes a loving, warmly human encounter with the Beloved and his continuing works. The presence of such a sympathy can go a long way toward guaranteeing simple historical accuracy, not to mention reinforcing the sense of causal relationships in what is studied.

For the traditionist, finally, the specific problem of interpreting Christian documents from the past is by no means an insuperable difficulty. True, his problems in establishing a reliable text and discovering what influences bore upon its composition are the same as anyone else's—but he is united in faith with the object described in such texts. He may not know all he wants to about the composition or the meaning of such texts, but he knows a great deal about the referent. Conversely, he knows to what extent various texts treat of the referent "Christ and the church," that is, he knows to which texts an assent of faith must be given. The difficulty is that the assent of faith seems to have to be given to ever more texts. There are texts from the past, of course, but there are also texts from the present purporting to be the sole authoritative interpretation of those perhaps looser texts from the past. It is in this manner that the historically researchable finally is integrated into dogmatics: in every conceivable turn of historical circumstance there is a text of the *magisterium,* assented to in faith, to guide one's assessment of circumstance. But the unsympathetic observer wonders whether this succession of interpretations ends by usurping the place of the human cultural development to which it is said to minister, if not, indeed, to inspire.

The great advantage of the gnostic approach is that it takes the human religious consciousness seriously. It must be emphasized, moreover, that the gnostic stress on human consciousness does not necessarily lead to what amounts to a kind of devotional solipsism. As Hegel shows in his posthumously published lectures on the philosophy of religion, the religious consciousness finds its truth precisely in and through its insertion into the history of human religious development. The Hegelian philosophy generally, and the Hegelian philosophy of religion, or gnosis, in particular are possible only on the soil of Protestant Christendom. Or better, they are not merely *possible*: they have actually occurred, just as Christendom itself. Modern gnosis is the most recent stage of a long development, and it could not have occurred without that development, without man's living-through of certain anterior and contributory stages of consciousness. Gnosis, then, as Baur goes to considerable pains to point out, is a meditation on faith, precisely *fides quaerens intellectum.* It presupposes faith, and what it knows is materially the same as what faith knows: it is a respectful improvement upon faith, not a substitute for it. As a learned discipline it does not fall into the only too common error of dissolving the data that are its justification! The preferability of gnosis over tradition, both for research and for life, lies in the fact that whereas tradition takes dogmas as first principles, gnosis searches for the first principles of dogmas. The respect of gnosis for the human self-consciousness lies therefore in its being a conscious, conceptualized, understanding of religious truth. The *whole* man, man exercising the fulness of his powers, religiously holds himself open and attentive to the self-manifestation of the absolute. Only gnosis is fully human religiosity.

In favor of the gnostic approach is the very considerable argument of fittingness to the effect that, after all, man is meant to live by his wits: capabilities are not granted in vain in a rational universe. In other words, the God of Hegelianism is conceived of as primarily benevolent, loving, self-communicative to man *as man happens to be,* not in a manner at variance with or disproportionate to, that is, *supernatural* to, man's powers. Or again, Hegelian gnosis emphasizes that the *revelation* of the mysteriousness of God is meant to make the absolute just a little less mysterious. The whole point of the dogma of the incarnation, for example, lies in the Johannine "he pitched his tent among us." In Hegel Luther's insistent "for us" reaches its full flowering: the passage from Christ's ubiquity to Christ's typological character (but typological just as a living, breathing, historical human being) *is made conscious.* Whereas (from the Hegelian point of view, at least), Schleiermacher's feeling of absolute dependence does not link the ideal and the historical Christ, precisely because it is, so to speak, cognitively dormant, what amounts to Hegel's doctrine of the necessity of the incarnation can make this link, precisely because it self-consciously, philosophically, knows that there must have been an "incarnation," a Christological moment, if you will, to account for man's present state of development. For the significance of the incarnation is simply that man began in a Christ to be what man now is and will become; in other words, there has to have been a historical beginning to historical man's present consciousness of the unity of the human with the divine nature, that is, of the participation, *consciously, or conceptually, apprehended,* of the human in the divine.

Now an obvious objection to the gnostic approach is that it refuses to accept certain classical Christian dogmas as literally true, that, as a result, it is incapable of really giving a satisfactory account of our fathers' faith, and that, therefore, it cannot demonstrate that it is the highest point in an allegedly continuous process of religious self-understanding. Does it not simply deny what the ages that led up to it held to be sacred truth? Does it not deny that there was once a historical individual called the Christ, the existence of which individual is attested by both faith and history, but primarily by faith, which individual had both a divine and a human nature and so was qualitatively different from any other mere man? Yes and no. What it really denies is that dogmas are any more than human, fallible interpretations of more basic *events*, that popes and bishops assembled count for as much as the redeemer that presumably commands their devotion. What it affirms is something that has become a commonplace of subsequent religious thought, namely, that revelation is primarily contained, not in words, but in the great deeds of God in history, in the *magnalia Dei,* as the Roman Liturgy used to say. What Baur wants is that Hegelian gnosis be taken seriously, that it be allowed to make a claim to being as profoundly religious as in fact it is. Hegel had no ambition to be another Voltaire: he despised what he considered the glib rationalism of the Enlightenment; in a letter to Tholuck Hegel stated that he was born a Lutheran and meant to die as one.[15] To the equally superficial literalisms of dogmatists and rationalists *datur tertium*: precisely in this middle way lies the only truly religious apprehension both of God's continuing creativity and of man's receptivity for it.

But there is a graver objection to the gnostic approach. The great disadvantage of this approach is its dependence upon a kind of secular faith in the rationality of the universe of its experience. No single point within this universe can any longer be held to be more than typologically Christological. It may be, of course, that once "nothing is sacred" everything is, but the multitudes that cry out for justice in every age seem to witness against this outlook. Christian gnosis treads a perilous path between moral insensitivity and the shattering of the humanistic faith upon which it depends.[16]

Quite evidently there are grave arguments both for and against each of the two approaches to the interpretation of the Christian past considered here. It must be emphasized that it has not been the intention of the present writer to award a prize either to Möhler the traditionist or Baur the gnostic, but only to catalogue the strengths and weaknesses of each position. It will not be out of place, however, to draw—or more exactly, *suggest*—two conclusions of a more limited and tentative nature.

What does Möhler's work suggest with respect to ecumenically inspired historical theology? If Möhler sometimes erred in his assessment of sixteenth-century opposed claims, it still can hardly be denied that his errors were those of a fundamentally well-informed critic. Quite apart from his apparent misunderstanding of the context of Protestant confessional definitions of the state of fallen man, Möhler saw very clearly that sixteenth-century opposed claims were in fact *opposed*. He saw, therefore, that passage from one set to the other could be mediated only by an outright conversion from ecclesiastical separatism, not by a theory of interpretation. His concept of living tradition is by no means meant to ensure Protestantism whatever rightful place it might have within the development of Christianity. The traditionist approach is rather designed to show that Protestantism is an untenable separatist aberration, and that the obvious good will of Protestants can find legitimate and joyful fulfillment only in the bosom of traditional Catholicism. This means conversion, as in the case of so many romantic thinkers and men of letters. This also means that reunion in terms of Schleiermacher's or—with reservations—Hegel's religious thought is a chimera:[17] the sometime opposites would be evacuated of positive content, and

---

[15]Hegel's actual words were, "Ich bin ein Lutheraner, und durch Philosophie ebenso ganz in Luthertum befestigt." *Briefe von und an Hegel,* ed. Johannes Hoffmeister and Rolf Flechsig, IV (Hamburg, 1961), 29.

[16]See Emil Fackenheim, *The Religious Dimension in Hegel's Thought* (Bloomington, Indiana, 1967), esp. pp. 235-42.

[17]The reservations are Möhler's, not Hegel's or Baur's—though even the latter two would oppose any other solution but the conversion of Catholics to *their* way of thinking. Contemporary neo-orthodox Protestants share Möhler's view of Hegel and Baur, as for example, Geiger, *op. cit.,* pp. 245ff., *even to the point of comparing Baur's teachings with the truths of the "gospel."* The gospel can doubtless fend for itself, but to blame Baur for not doing what it would have been illogical for him to do makes for confusing intellectual history.

such reunion as might occur would be based on indifference to the past. Clearly this would be less a reunion than a mass apostasy. The lesson contained in Möhler's contribution to this controversy is that an honest attempt at the reunion of the confessions must go back, as far as possible, and resolve the opposed claims; Catholics and Protestants alike must re-examine the roles of pope and emperor in German political and economic life, the encounter of Luther with Cardinal Cajetan, the tragic breaking off of the Colloquy of Regensburg. By taking the position of, in effect, defending Protestantism from Baur, Möhler eloquently affirmed that in interconfessional relations no *theory of interpretation* can substitute for accurate historical research, for any theory that would proclaim the unimportance of past controversies proclaims in the same words the unimportance of the very basis and motivation of the confessions to be reunited. And Möhler's own lapses from historical probity need only be a stimulus to future enquirers.

Möhler's concept of traditional Catholicism, moreover, quite consciously de-emphasizes some of the principal stumbling blocks that Protestants find in Catholicism. Möhler, who had died well before mounting political and ideological challenges led Catholics to clamor for a strong papacy, is no friend of the papal-monarchy conception of the church; the hand of the historian is evident here! Möhler, who is very sympathetic with the Jansenist movement, never fails to point out that man's reason needs divine assistance to come to the knowledge of God and that man's will can only respond to divine initiatives, with the very response being a divine gift. The student of the patristic period (in his two earlier books, *Die Einheit in der Kirche* and *Athanasius der Grosse*) gives relatively little notice to the *impedimenta* of medieval folk-piety, and tends to refer doctrinal differences to the area of Christology, where agreement might be more easily arrived at. (Justification by faith as opposed to justification by love is taken up in relation to the offices of Christ: priest, king, *and teacher*.) Möhler endeavors at every turn to point out that Catholic doctrine is psychologically satisfying to man's legitimate aspirations, even while holding man in constant moral reckoning before God. Conversion may be called for, but the conversion to Catholicism that Möhler envisages is scarcely a violent one—and its way is smoothed by historical research. What Möhler does not want is a unity founded on subjective whim (which he regards as characteristic of the religiosity of Schleiermacher and Hegel); what he does hope for is unity founded upon the *objective history* of western Christendom, as seen in the power of the Spirit.

To turn now to Baur, what does his work suggest as to the nature of historical theology, not as a kind of self-contained world, but as a humane discipline?

With respect to the Christian past and the divisions within it Baur wants not only to feel or to believe but understand. Now there is a sense in which Schleiermacher's thought—which Baur profoundly modified for himself—is very like that of Möhler. Both Schleiermacher and Möhler attempt to pull together an irrational source of religion and an empirical study of the Christian communal consciousness. Baur's basic criticism of them both is that *they slight reason*. And *reason* here means both the enquiring reason of the historian and the speculative reason of the metaphysician; the Baur who embraced Hegelian gnosis is the same Baur who as a young classics teacher immersed himself in both the great classical historians and the great Barthold Niebuhr.[18] Baur's gnosis will always be somewhat misunderstood if it is seen as a gratuitous superstructure imposed on Christian history. It is a serious attempt to render history coherently meaningful *precisely as history*, to hold together categories of understanding and the liveliness of the events to be understood. No matter what attitude one may take toward traditionist faith, one must concede to Baur the point illustrated in his first large-scale discussion of confessional differences, namely, that research in the history of doctrine tends (whether rightly or wrongly is another matter) to generate overviews of a metaphysical nature.

Between, therefore, what Möhler once termed the *chronique scandaleuse* of Enlightenment church history and Möhler's own fundamentally supernatural linking of the details of Christian history, *datur tertium*. Hegelian gnosis, as already noted, arises for both the individual and the collectivity out of the inspection of historical fact (that is, the experiment one is invited to make in taking the *Phenomenology* seriously). Every historical theologian, traditionists included, must come to terms with the problem of historical generalizations and inferences. As Baur himself saw, therefore, even the most anti-traditionist Protestant historical theologian is compelled by the mere fact of being a historian to develop some sense of linkage between disparate events, to develop, in a word, a feeling for tradition—in the context of ecclesiastical doctrine and life, ecclesiastical tradition. On the other hand, both Catholics and Protestants are driven back to a detailed examination of the Reformation period by the need to see if it be at all possible to reconceptualize (without denaturing) the facts in terms of a wider understanding of tradition or continuity. (After all, it is scarcely possible for any historically-minded person to insist that something that has lasted several centuries, like Protestantism, has no *raison d'etre*.) And just as with Möhler, Baur's factual errors need deter no one from attempting to do better.

Another way of stating Baur's contribution to historical theology is to point out that he was among the first, if not the first, to apply to Christian history the methods of historical study that Niebuhr and other secular scholars like him had developed for their own fields. Baur's work has, as a result, a dual, if somewhat paradoxical effect. As has been pointed out, Baur insists that the history of Christianity obey the same rules as the history of anything else. In so doing he emerges—along with, though very much more than, Schleiermacher—as a forerunner of those who in the twentieth century would see in historical theology a sub-division of humane studies generally. On the other hand, by insisting on

[18]See Hodgson, *op. cit.*, pp. 169f., n. 89; also Klaus Scholder, "Ferdinand Christian Baur als Historiker," *Evangelische Theologie*, XXI (1961), 435-48.

being simultaneously both a historian and a theologian, Baur raises a very important question for present-day humane studies, and particularly for history.

As Baur neared death most of his contemporaries dismissed him as the crazy old man down in Tübingen who had opened a sort of Pandora's box of unbelief and then was embarrassed about it: they never forgave him the Strauss affair. Still, both they—and we—might conceivably be guilty of a kind of loss of nerve before the gnostic synthesis that Baur championed.[19] Such a synthesis, as has been noted, is something of a scandal for the human mind.

It was suggested above that an abiding lesson of Baur's work is that research in the history of doctrine does often—and perhaps one can say *tends to*—generate overviews of a metaphysical nature. Now Baur, because he was a theologian, felt not only free but impelled, so to speak, to call a spade a spade: if coherence in a historical account of Christian doctrine and life called for a metaphysics of the absolute and of human freedom (from immediacy), Baur did what was called for and called what he did by its right name—gnosis. Baur ended up keeping to a peculiar sort of middle way. If from the standpoint of orthodoxy—Catholic or Protestant—he was too much a metaphysician, from the standpoint of many present-day historically-minded observers he is *still* too much a metaphysician. To Möhler Baur seemed an odd sort of theologian—to be precise, a knight in an 1833 frock coat. To the twentieth-century reader Baur may well seem an odd sort of historian—but there, precisely, lies the continuing

---

[19]The thought is Karl Barth's, in *From Rousseau to Ritschl,* tr. B. Cozens (London, 1959), pp. 279ff.

[20]The question raised here is (a) much more a twentieth than a nineteenth-century matter, and (b) much more a matter of what might be termed "philosophy of history" than historiography itself. Twentieth-century analytical observations about historiographical statements (about which see, for example, Arthur C. Danto, *Analytical Philosophy of History* [Cambridge, 1968], pp. 34-62) have the effect of "raising the ante" for the historian: *either* historiographical statements are in fact elaborately complicated statements *about the present*—and hence not historiographical at all—*or* the historiographer, at least to make sense to himself as a serious researcher, must establish principles that are in effect a modest venture into metaphysics. To put it another way, from problems arising out of the inspection of historical propositions one is led to inquire about the meaning of history as a humane discipline; and inquiry into the meaning of history-as-a-humane-discipline leads to inquiry into the meaning of history-as-object-studied. Of course, the historian is entitled simply to stick to his business and let someone else worry about whether his business is or is not to be a purveyor of fairy-tales. But if the historian be inclined to do his own worrying, he may find the example of Baur instructive. However much one might be inclined to quarrel with Baur's Hegelian philosophy of history, one must grant that at least he *had* a philosophy of history, and apparently felt the need to state it explicitly. Baur felt such a need, it would seem, because he was a *theologian* doing history; the question of the *philosophy* of history touches Baur because Baur's theology was a theology, so he claimed, stabilized by metaphysics. Regarding the point of departure for all this transcendental worrying, namely, the suspicion that empirical philosophy might not be so empirical as it looks, see R. G. Collingwood, *The Principles of Art* (New York, 1958), "The Theory of Imagination," pp. 155-269. See also *idem, An Autobiography* (Oxford, 1939), esp. pp. 29ff.

interest of Baur's work. Twentieth-century history is often unsure of the meta-physical status of its generalizations and inferences, often burdened with unexamined hypotheses—metaphysical wolves in empirical clothing.[20] Baur stated as the glory of Protestant theological research its openness to the absolute; it was this theological, or if you will, metaphysical, stance that enabled him to be both candid and lucid as to the nature of his generalizations and inferences. Occasionally he got the facts wrong, but whether he had a more solid grasp of the nature of historical research than some of his latter-day colleagues is at least an open question. What he pioneered was a kind of mutuality between theology and the humanities. The humanities contribute their method.[21] Theology contributes certain recurrent traits of the believer—no matter how it may subsequently dissect the nature of belief. There is the believer's need for an absolute that is causally related to human dealings. There is also the believer's sympathy for the history of his community, as well as his need for a coherent basis on which to continue to deal with fellow man. Unless one is resigned to dismissing human affairs as "one damn thing after another," these are precious gifts for the humanities.

It is hardly problematic to affirm that the working methods of the historian are adequate for the attainment of historical conclusions. (It is almost tautologi-cal.) But this is not the question here. Rather, to be carried out coherently and satisfyingly, not by a kind of abstract historian, but *by a human being,* as an element in the achievement, not merely of academic ends, but of human, indeed, religious ends, does the study of history intrinsically demand to be carried out in the context of a metaphysics? This is one salient question among the many questions put to our time by the crazy old man in Tübingen, who wanted to be a real historian and a real theologian *at the same time.*[22]

Ecumenically-minded historical theologians may opt either for faith or for philosophy of religion as court of last resort. But they can never successfully opt against the effort to resolve opposed claims. Neither can they ignore the fact that the history of doctrine generates new, co-ordinating doctrine. No matter what else it accomplished,[23] the Möhler-Baur controversy clearly figured forth these constants of symbolical and historical theology.

[21]For the sake of brevity *method* is here used to suggest the variety of ways in which historians, literary critics, political scientists, etc., go about their work. Baur's work, how-ever, should be seen as continuing that of Lessing and Schleiermacher, if not also that of the English Deists.

[22]That history cannot take the place of metaphysics, or metaphysical theology, and *vice versa,* would not seem to preclude a certain parallelism of awarenesses: in Baur's view history generates co-ordinating doctrine, whereas doctrine is never to be permitted to lose sight of its historical point of departure. The crux of the matter is that, to the Hegelian mentality, "metaphysics" is not mere "theory" but the highest level of historical reality or actualization.

[23]The controversy actually accomplished a great deal. Writing in 1885, Heinrich Kihn (of Würzburg University) remarked of his youth that Möhler's *Symbolik* "made it an honor

again to be a Catholic." (In J. M. Raich, ed., *Ergänzungen zu Möhler's Symbolik* [Mainz, 1902], p. 1.) Möhler's work can be seen as part of a two-level effort at the revitalization of German Catholicism—and the effort was in large part successful. At the level of political-social action, and just shortly after the *Symbolik,* came the successful resistance of Clemens-August zu Droste-Vischering, Archbishop of Cologne, to Prussian policies on marriage laws and clerical education. Again and again in retrospective literature, the *Symbolik* and the *Kölner Ereignis* receive emphatic mention.